ITALY
Through The Rear-View Mirror

FINDING CONNECTION AND BELONGING

SUSAN J. BOCOCK

Tellwell Talent
www.tellwell.ca

ISBN
978-0-2288-4449-5 (Paperback)
978-0-2288-4448-8 (eBook)

MAP OF ITALY

TABLE OF CONTENTS

REGIONS, CAPITALS, AND PLACES

Northern Regions

Aosta Valley (Aosta)
Courmayeur, Gran Paradiso

Piedmont (Turin)
Alba, Asti, Alessandria, Barolo, Casale Monferrato, Cella Monte, Ottiglio, Vignale Monferrato
 ❖ La Casaccia Winery and Agriturismo

Liguria (Genoa)
Campiglia, Cinque Terre, Monterosso al Mare, Vernazza, Riomaggiore, Portovenere

Lombardy (Milan)
Como

Trentino Alto Adige (Trento)
Bolzano, Merano, Tre Cime di Lavaredo

Veneto (Venice)
Murano, Burano, Verona, Malcesine, Monte Baldo, Riva del Garda.

Friuli Venezia Giulia (Trieste)
Sappada

Emilia-Romagna (Bologna)
Parma, Ravenna

Central Regions

Lazio (Rome)

Bolsena, Campodimele, Capodimonte, Cellere, Circeo National Park, Civita di Bagnoregio, Civitavecchia, Fiumicino, Fondi, Gaeta, Lake Bolsena, Lenola, Marta, Monte Cassino, Montefiascone, Monte San Biagio, Norma, Ostia, Ostia Antica, Parco di Vulci, Pontecorvo, Ponza Is., San Felice Circeo, Saturnia, Scarlino, Sperlonga, Tarquinia, Tuscania, Terracina, Vallecorsa, Viterbo

❖   Gatta Morena B&B

Marche (Ancona)

Tuscany (Florence)

Bagno Vignoni, Capalbio, Capraia Is., Castellina in Chianti, Elba Is., Greve in Chianti, Lucca, Montalcino, Montepulciano, Monteriggioni, Monte Amiato, Monte Capanne, Palazzone, Panzano, Pienza, Pisa, Pitigliano, Porto Azzurro, San Casciano dei Bagni, Siena, San Gimignano

❖   Agriturismo Il Colle

Umbria (Perugia)

Orvieto

Abruzzo (L'Aquila)

Campo Imperatore, Gran Sasso National Park

Molise (Campobasso)

Southern Regions

Campania (Naples)
Capri, Anacapri, Herculaneum, Monte Solaro, Mount Vesuvius, Pompeii, Salerno

Apulia (Bari)
Alberobello, Brindisi, Gallipoli, Lecce, Monopoli, Otranto, Ostuni, Roseto Valfortore, Santa Maria di Leuca, Soleto, Vieste, Zollino

Basilicata (Potenza)
Matera

Calabria (Catanzaro)
Reggio di Calabria

Sicily (Palermo)
Agrigento, Castelmola, Catania, Cefalù, Delia, Isola Bella, Mount Etna, Noto, Pachino, San Marzano sul Sarno, Taormina, Trapani

Sardinia (Cagliari)
Alghero, Asinara Is., Borutta, Bosa, Capo Caccia, Costa Paradiso, Monti del Gennargentu, Monte San Giovanni, Nuoro, Oristano, Orgosolo, Porto Conto, Porto Ferro, Sant'Antioco (Is. and city), Sassari, Stintino
   ❖ B&B Rosy in Campania

ACKNOWLEDGMENTS

This book is a tribute to all those who fed and supported my love of Italy and my desire to write about it. In particular, I want to thank my husband Gord for being my companion and biggest supporter throughout much of my travels, our dear friends Joe and Filomena, whose generosity opened Italy up to me in ways that would otherwise not have been possible, family and friends who added to the joy I found in Italy, my aunt, Tina Pentland, for her dedication to editing this manuscript and providing valuable suggestions that only improved the book, my sister for her technical assistance, and my mom for always making me feel like I could do anything I set my mind to.

PREFACE

I consider myself relatively conservative by nature. At least I thought I was. But reflecting on my adventures exploring all corners of Italy, and how I searched for every possible way to stretch my travel dollars and extend my stays, I was forced to revisit that assumption. Perhaps I am in fact more of a risk-taker than I thought. Or perhaps my inexplicable passion for Italy allowed me to override any inherent fears and to live out my dreams, one Italian region at a time. Either way, the journey has forever changed me.

This book began as an effort to share real-life experiences from travels through the twenty regions of Italy with those who have an interest in Italy, a zest for travel, and a yearning to pursue their passions. It continues to fulfill that commitment, but as I scratched beneath the surface it turned into so much more.

Before you turn another page, I want to be clear about what this book is not. You will not find highlights of the best places to visit in each of Italy's twenty regions or lists of the top ten things to see and do. Certainly, you will read about fascinating places and learn something of the geography and history of Italy; but you will discover, as I did, that those are just the backdrop for a more meaningful narrative.

As I pursued my passion, Italy and its inhabitants helped me discover the real reasons behind my growing attachment to this sun-drenched Mediterranean country, and what the drive behind my dream of exploring its twenty regions was really about. At some point it was no longer a question of if, but when I would get to all of them. I focused my vacation time on Italy, convincing my husband to come along when he could, and together we spent more and more time abroad. My extended travels often took me off the beaten path. Though not entirely by design, this served me well. Where I went, and when, was a rather organic process. At times I toured with friends or family, depending on their availability and interests. I was happy to return to the places I loved, over and over in some cases, getting something more out of each experience.

I also explored diverse interests of my own, including participating in a yoga retreat in the southern region of Apulia and working as a volunteer at an *agriturismo* (working farm) in the northern region of Piedmont. I reached out to friends and family of Italians I knew, who were scattered throughout the peninsula and on three of Italy's main islands. I set off in search of small towns and rustic experiences I heard about from locals and sought out cool-looking places I came across on the internet. As the stories will show, it was often out-of-the-way places and lesser-known attractions (the ones that people don't necessarily go to Italy to visit) that offered the greatest rewards. As years passed, I managed to find an 'excuse' to travel to Italy almost every summer for fifteen years. *Molto fortunata lo so!* Very lucky, I know!

So, what then is the essence of the book I felt itching to get out of me as my Italian experiences mounted? I knew there was something far beyond Italy's picturesque landscape and miles of beaches that was drawing me back year after year. Beneath the obvious beauty, amazing food, and spectacular cultural and historical sites, there was something more building my sense of connection to a country I otherwise had no connection with. And although I have been imagining this book for several years, it took what felt like an eternity to figure out what that 'something' was.

Then one day I picked up a book by the inspirational speaker and writer, Brené Brown. It was about connection and belonging, a surprising place to find the theme I had been unable to articulate. But there it was. As Brown put it, 'We are different in many ways, but underneath it all we are deeply connected.' I was going to have to do a lot more reading to understand why, but I knew instantly that this sentence spoke directly to the hold Italy had on me. I also knew that while Italy was my teacher, and the vehicle that helped me understand how deeply we are all connected, that undeniable sense of connection was the more compelling story I wanted to explore.

My travel blogs created a foundation for this book. Stories were supplemented through research and from conversations with those involved. I prepared a chronology, which provided a challenge of its own, albeit an enjoyable one—figuring out the when and where, the who and the what. The process was illuminating. It reminded me of details I had forgotten, and at the same time provided a bird's eye view of the bigger picture the stories were telling. This wider lens opened my eyes to how traditional and everyday aspects of Italian life that I had been experiencing throughout my travels were fostering a sense of belonging—the ties that were binding it together for me, and me to it.

Had I started writing years ago, when I first began visiting Italy, this would have been an entirely different book, if written at all. I simply did not know then what I know now. But as is often the case with the benefit of hindsight, I am now connecting the dots. That 'something' is now shouting at me. And I am listening.

I'm convinced that comparable experiences (and lessons) can be found wherever we choose to travel, if we are willing to open our hearts and embrace what we find. In the interim, and as I wait with you for that opportunity to travel again, I hope you will join me for a journey that took me from a wide-eyed child to a fifty-something, attracted at first by the beauty and diversity of the country, only to realize by the time I had explored every region that the attraction had much more to do with their similarities than their differences, and the people much more than the places. Particularly at times when our capacity to travel is limited and our ability to connect feels distant, the message is more relevant than ever. It will inspire those with a desire to cultivate authentic relationships along their journey, whether that involves travel or not, and in the process learn about our connection to this global community we call humanity. In uncertain times, there is always the option of travelling vicariously, from the comfort of your own home. Whatever you choose, the rewards will be waiting.

INTRODUCTION

One way or another, I think we are all destined to learn
the same lessons in life. Universal truths are universal
truths.

—Richelle E. Goodrich

I am not Italian, although friends would joke that I must have
been in another life, as they pushed their wine glasses out of
reach of my waving hands. But a lack of Italian ancestry did not
prevent me from developing a passion for Italy that has profoundly
shaped my life. For whatever reason, Italy kept pulling me back.
As W. H. Hudson concluded after journeying to the outer
reaches of Patagonia in the 1860s, 'Desert wanderers discover
within themselves a primaeval calmness, which is perhaps the
same as the Peace of God.' Similarly, North American Indians
went to their mountains to find their spirit. I related to these
sentiments. My energy was different in Italy. In a place many
might generously describe as chaotic, I found a deeper sense
of calm; an ability to exhale. I felt more present, even more so
than in my morning meditations or the many yoga classes I have
taken and taught. I felt a freedom to live a fuller, richer, more
authentic life.

Perhaps a seed was planted my first time in Italy. I was
ten and my dad wanted to buy an Italian car in Milan. My
recollections are not so much of the details, but of my feelings
and impressions from that visit. I remember being fascinated
by the strange-sounding Italian language, and the charming
accent of Italians struggling to speak English. I remember the
exotic look of the tall, dark-eyed man behind the counter at the
airport, talking passionately with his hands as customers came

and went. I remember the flaky *cornetto con cioccolato*, and those tiny coffee cups.

That seed has been fed by various experiences since, to a point where I wanted to spend every holiday in Italy. My lofty goal was challenging since I live across the pond in Canada, but I found ways to make it happen. I also wanted to learn the language (a work in progress), to hang out in Italian cafes, and I always looked for the Little Italy neighbourhood of cities I visited. At some point along this journey, it struck me that I needed to visit every region of Italy, all twenty of them. That became *il sogno* (the dream).

When people asked me what I loved about Italy, I would recount the feelings and emotions it elicited. I loved the pulse of life I felt in the streets, the parks and piazzas, and the cafes. I cherished the reliability of cloudless summer skies and the warmth that the Mediterranean climate offered. I welcomed greetings from shopkeepers and neighbours. Other than perhaps afternoon *riposo* (siesta) and family meals, it seemed that much of Italian life happens outdoors, in its public spaces. The piazza can leave you wondering if you are at home in your living room, and a trip to the local cafe feels like a visit with friends. Neighbours hang out on their balconies chatting endlessly across narrow streets and alleys, some even gathering on the sidewalk. My best recollection of this is in Fondi (Lazio), where I have stayed numerous times. Every morning without fail, or at least in the warmer months when I was visiting, and often every evening, a group of neighbours would drag their plastic chairs out onto the street corner to socialise and watch the world go by. It was their version of going out for coffee and *aperitivo* (a pre-dinner drink), just without beverages or a trip to the local cafe.

As cafes and stores re-open in late afternoon, people stop on their way home from work or emerge from their houses, ready to shop, meet friends for a drink, or perhaps enjoy a gelato with their kids. On weekends they wander downtown for evening *passeggiata*—that quintessentially Italian evening stroll—and to meet up with friends. They congregate on the steps of the *chiesa* after celebrating baptisms, weddings, lives passed, and parade in the streets for saints' days and festivals. In contrast to the more socially restrained culture I grew up in, their lives seemed more tethered to social interaction, centred around friends and extended family, and their many religious and social rituals. Through these time-honoured traditions, Italians cultivate and embrace their connections, turning towards each other rather than away, finding any reason to celebrate family and community—'living life in the piazza' as I like to say.

But why did I find this all so appealing, almost addictive? I discovered from further reading that there may in fact be scientific and physiological reasons behind the attraction. I am anything but a science nerd, but what I read intuitively made sense. These examples of in-person interactions that I loved about Italy are what Brown refers to as 'collective assembly', which she says meets a primal human yearning for shared social experiences. She adds, 'Not only do moments of collective emotion remind us of what is possible between people, they also remind us of what is true about the human spirit—we are all wired for connection.'

Brown's quote made me think of Frances, Diane Lane's character in the movie *Under the Tuscan Sun*. When the story begins, Frances may not have realized what she was looking for when moving to Italy, but to my mind this is exactly what she ended up with by the time her derelict Tuscan villa, Bramasole, was restored—an amazing feeling of connection and family and belonging. I knew there was a reason I liked that movie!

Intrigued, I did more digging. My research has meandered rather erratically, but it has also presented some solutions to my dangling participles. Take Maslow's hierarchy of needs. How I got onto that topic escapes me, but I found it enlightening. Maslow believed that fundamental physiological needs (food, water, and shelter) must be satisfied before we will be motivated to achieve what he saw as higher-level needs, such as those related to social belonging (friendships, family, intimate relationships). That said, more recent research, such as that of developmental psychologist Susan Pinker and social psychologist Matthew Lieberman, support a contrary view—that humans are hard-wired for connection, and that social bonds are a fundamental human need essential for our survival.

On the issue of what we need to get us through more challenging times, I stumbled on an interesting phenomenon referred to as the Roseto Effect. Unlike anywhere else in the United States, residents of the Pennsylvania borough of Roseto were one hundred percent Italian, the vast majority from Roseto Valfortore in southern Italy. What drew scientists to this otherwise unremarkable town was that its mortality rate from heart attacks was roughly half that of other towns in the area. After several years of study, where diet, age, occupation, income level, and every other conceivable explanation was ruled out, researchers were left with only one possibility: Rosetans were less susceptible to heart disease than their neighbours because they maintained their traditional way of life and strong family and community relationships. Despite eating a high cholesterol diet, working in heavy industry, smoking stogies, and drinking wine, Roseto was populated by closely knit Italian American families who nourished and supported each other in good and bad times.

This theory was bolstered by later studies demonstrating an almost perfect correlation between the Americanisation of Roseto (meaning less close, less modest, less interdependent) and death rates due to heart disease. The magic ingredient had been family and community support that allowed Rosetans to manage stress more effectively. The progressive dismantling of social ties, growing conspicuous consumption by those with wealth, marriages outside the Italian community, and lack of adherence to common values eroded the Roseto Effect. Within a decade of the first study, the town experienced heart disease on par with every other town in America.

In the same vein, Pinker discusses why the secret to living longer is less dependent on one's diet, or numerous other factors commonly associated with longevity, and more linked to one's social life. In *The Village Effect*, she described her research on the island of Sardinia, where there are apparently ten times as many centenarians as in North America, and even six times as many as on the Italian mainland. She identified two key factors to longevity—close personal relationships and in-person connections.

Because of the conventional design of their ancient towns, the lives of the villagers she studied constantly intersected. With their narrow, interwoven alleys and tightly spaced houses confined by protective medieval walls, residents were more likely to have face-to-face social interaction and close, long-term, relationships. They were impossible to avoid. And while the physical limitations of these ancient villages helped create an environment conducive to social interaction, Pinker also witnessed an important social network where residents were surrounded by extended family, friends, and neighbours throughout life. These factors combined to form what she referred to as their 'personal village'. As with the close-knit network in Roseto, villagers were rarely left to live solitary lives, and were healthier for it.

I came across this theme in other places as well—that social connection is a bigger predictor of physical and psychological well-being, including longevity and happiness, than factors such as obesity and high blood pressure. Something as simple as smiling, making eye contact, or shaking hands can have a positive neurological impact on our body's chemistry, increasing levels of trust and lowering stress. It doesn't seem to matter whether the interaction is with family or mere acquaintances, as much as how integrated you are socially and how much you interact with people throughout your day.

Through the rear-view mirror, I'm wondering if this might be the reason it didn't matter that I was not connecting with family in Italy. I was connecting, and that was what counted. And if this is not enough, even the Dalai Lama has pointed out on many occasions that we are all social animals, and our happiness depends on our community.

So, how does all this social connection talk relate to my travels through Italy? Quite simply, it made the tug I was feeling make sense—like finding the missing piece of a puzzle that has monopolised your dining table for far too long. What I found in Italy was a culture of community and social interaction beyond anything I had experienced previously. And my unscientific conclusion is that I have been experiencing what Pinker describes as the 'biological imperative' we all possess to know that we belong. The point is not that I belong in Italy, though the idea is appealing. Rather, the opportunities my trips to Italy afforded me to interact and connect with locals in some very personal ways fed that biological quest. Like all of us, I am wired for connection.

Elderly ladies in a narrow street in Sperlonga, Lazio

CHAPTER 1

L'Inizio – The Beginning

Open my heart and you will see, engraved inside of it,
Italy.

—Robert Browning

My introduction to Italy as an adult was during a trip to Switzerland, when we decided to visit the city of Lugano in Ticino, a predominantly Italian-speaking canton of Switzerland. Bordered by Italy to the south and west, and with its palm trees, beaches, and piazzas, Ticino has a Mediterranean flair characteristic of Italy. Its architecture, culture, and cuisine are also heavily influenced by its neighbour to the south. We arrived in mid-April, wanting to see palm trees and hopefully experience the warm winds, characteristic of the region, that can rapidly make a mild spring day feel like summer. I was again drawn to people speaking Italian in the streets, and during a boat excursion on Lake Lugano I remember our guide noting that we had crossed the invisible border into Italy. I loved the idea that we were in *bella Italia* and thought how amazing it would be to return for a 'real' visit.

My next Italian connection came when I started playing soccer (as we call European football in North America). The sport was new to me, but I was immediately hooked, and I met a few Italians, not a surprise given their enthusiasm for the sport. I also started playing drop-in soccer with a co-ed group that included several Italians. We almost always headed to the same Italian restaurant after our games. I enjoyed the connection, both over soccer and over a glass of *vino*. Here I learned about pizza with capers and anchovies (not my favourite), *caffè corretto* (espresso 'corrected' with a liqueur such as Sambuca), and a few Italian swear words thrown in for good measure. I also started hanging out at an Italian cafe in a part of Edmonton affectionately known as Little Italy. It was captivating to watch retired men come in daily *per un caffè,* arguing in Italian while they played with their funny-looking cards. This was a scene I would come to see enacted in Italy many times.

I was enchanted by the language too. I studied French in school but had not heard or spoken it for years after moving out west to a predominantly non-bilingual area of Canada. As a Latin-based language it did, however, give me a leg-up for learning Italian. I joined an Italian conversation group and started taking evening classes at the university. Both helped me learn the basics and continued to build my intrigue for all things Italian. And perhaps most importantly, I was introduced to my first Italian teacher. Her enthusiasm for teaching us the language was matched by her desire to expose us to everything about Italy, from its food to its politics. I even experienced my first traditional Italian Christmas dinner thanks to Antonella, who hosted our entire class. We feasted on traditional Italian dishes, sang Italian Christmas songs, and learned about *La Befana*, Italy's version of Santa Claus who brings treats to all good children on the morning of Epiphany. To my mind, this all helped nurture the seed planted in me as a child.

By now I was hooked, and a trip to Italy became my next focus. I was fortunate to get a taste test during a side trip on a vacation to Germany. The beauty of Lake Como, in the northern region of Lombardy, coupled with my first experience of an Italian *mercato* (market) and an outdoor screening of a

World Cup game of soccer (where mass celebrations broke out in the streets following Italy's win) only enhanced my expectations. The next year, after several planning meetings, which naturally involved pasta and vino, Gord and I joined a group of friends for a holiday in Tuscany.

The renowned beauty of the Tuscan countryside speaks for itself, but the warmth of the Italians I met, including the owners of the villa we rented, became another lure. Our hosts graciously invited us into their home, where I saw ancient frescos on their ceilings and a hand-blown Venetian glass chandelier hanging in their living room. Maria cursed that her 93-year-old mother-in-law would not let her change a thing in the historic home. As a result, she had resigned herself to doing much of her cooking in the original wood-burning oven. Her husband, Giacomo, showed us where he made olive oil, including a huge stone wheel used to crush olives in the 1600s, and we toured the *cantina* (cellar) where his family produced Chianti Classico. Yes, it was their business, but they could not have been more welcoming, and the passion with which they shared their work, their traditions, even their home, stayed with me.

Talking about this visit to Tuscany reminds me of a funny story. While waiting to meet Giacomo in a tiny dot on the map called Palazzone, I noticed two men sitting on a bench in the *piazzetta*, or little piazza. The next night our group returned for dinner at the only restaurant in town, and there they were again. In my best Italian at that time, I asked, *Ancora qui?* Here again? Their response? *Sempre qui!* We are always here! This tradition was something I would come to appreciate as a common occurrence throughout Italy. Why sit at home when you can be outside with friends, reliving yesterday's football game, or just watching the world go by?

The more regions I travelled through, the more my desire grew to visit others. At the outset I was drawn to the beauty and the diversity that Italy offered. Miles of beaches and snow-capped mountains. Vineyards, orchards and olive groves framed by cypress trees reaching for the sky. Quaint fishing villages with *pescatori* displaying their early morning catch. Medieval hilltop towns with their walled *centro storico* (historic centre), and cities full of history and culture and vibrancy at the same time. And while the extraordinary diversity added to the allure, the more I saw, the more I began to appreciate the similarities as well.

CHAPTER 2

Quanto Costa? –
How Much Does It Cost?

The cost of a thing is the amount of what I will call life which is required to be exchanged for it.
—Henry David Thoreau

While drafting this book, I was coincidentally sent an article explaining the principles that make up poet and philosopher Henry David Thoreau's 'new economics', as it was called. Written by Dan Hugger, a researcher at the Acton Institute, the article noted that Thoreau's rigor in applying these economic insights to his own life 'still inspires many today to think through what matters most and to count the costs'.

Thoreau's concept made sense to me as I reflected on choices I had made relating to my travels. Being infatuated with Italy and having a desire to spend as much time there as possible was not the same as having the financial means or the freedom to do so. Choices had to be made. While I fully acknowledge my own good fortune in having the means to explore Italy from top to bottom and recognise that much of that has to do with the reality that I was lucky enough to be born into, there is also an aspect of values and choices that play into the equation.

In his book, *Onward*, Howard Schultz (then CEO of the world-famous Starbucks company) writes about choices he had to make during his Starbucks journey that went against common sense and 'the wise counsel of people we trust'. He says that we proceed 'despite the risks and rational argument', because we believe in our chosen path and because 'we refuse to be bystanders, even if we do not know exactly where our actions will lead'. Schultz suggests that this is 'the kind of passionate conviction that sparks romances, wins battles, and drives people to pursue dreams others wouldn't dare'. He also quotes the adage, 'Life is a sum of all your choices' (attributed to Albert Camus), which encapsulates his own view that 'large or small, our actions forge our futures'.

These comments resonated with me in several ways. No, I was not making life-and-death decisions when I chose to spend my time and money on travel; nor was I making choices that were going to impact the life of a multimillion-dollar corporation. Nevertheless, I was making important decisions relative to pursuing the life I hoped for myself. Schultz's words made me more appreciative of the life I had, one that afforded me the luxury of such choices and opportunities, and I was determined to make the most of them.

Perhaps the most significant choice I made regarding finances was to enrol in an employee-funded leave program at work. The program involved deferring a portion of my salary for two or more years, after which I could take paid leave of up to six months. It effectively reduced my annual income by about twenty percent for the eight or so years I was enrolled, since my leave pay was simply repayment of the salary I had deferred while working. My choice was to forfeit a portion of my income and open myself up to new opportunities. In return I was rewarded with significantly more 'free' time, which itself was incredibly liberating, and hence more time to travel. The chunk of my life this choice returned to me, that allowed me to explore my passions rather than heading to the office five days a week, was, as they say, priceless.

My next question became: How much time could I afford to spend in Italy? The intrinsic value of the experiences grew with each transcontinental trip, as did my determination to find ways to return sooner, and for longer. I was fortunate to have a supportive husband who knew what travel (particularly to Italy) meant to me and never questioned this allocation of our discretionary income. On the contrary, he often joined me on my adventures, and on other occasions (such as when I was sitting on a curb in tears after a mini meltdown, or just feeling too far away from home), he was my long-distance confidant.

A couple of years ago I was staying at a B&B in Sardinia, owned by my now friend Rosanna. I have more to say about my time with her, but here I want to talk about a discussion we got into with one of her friends who worked at a nearby university. She was an educated, intelligent woman with a good job, but her view was that most Italian people, herself included, could not afford to travel as I did, for example, or have a large house with land as Rosanna did. Rosanna and I both agreed without argument that we are indeed privileged, and we understood that there are many people who will never be able to afford to travel or own their own home. I get that. But among those who can make choices, there are options. In my case, I can afford to travel in part because we intentionally don't have a big house or fancy new cars. In Rosanna's case, she has a larger house but doesn't travel much. She also uses her home as a bed and breakfast to supplement her income, in addition to being extremely self-sufficient, growing much of what she eats, making her own olive oil, and so forth. As my favourite travel writer Rick Steves says, 'Affordable travel is a matter of priorities. (Make do with the old sofa.)'

The point is that, at whatever level, we all make choices. If we know what our passion is, the choices can seem obvious. It still may not be easy, but we will better understand the costs.

CHAPTER 3

Il Seme – The Seed

Italy is a dream that keeps returning for the rest of your life.

—Anna Akhmatova

My father decided to buy a Fiat, and he wanted to go right to the source to get it. His idea was to pick the car up in Milan, drive to Hungary to spend Christmas with family, and then head back to Milan and have the car shipped home. Where this idea came from, or why I was the one of three siblings who went along, I don't know, but off we went. The trip was definitely an eye-opener.

After sorting out paperwork, we hopped into our shiny new *macchina* and drove east, making it as far as Verona before stopping for the night. In the morning we were shocked to discover that our new car had been broken into (too shiny perhaps?) and my father's winter coat stolen. To add insult to injury, we headed the wrong way on the *autostrada*, going back towards Milan instead of east towards Venice. If you have been on Italy's major highways you will know that exit points can be few and far between. There were some choice words from my dad, but eventually we got back on track.

We passed Venice and starting to climb into the mountains north of Trieste, the regional capital of Friuli Venezia Giulia. Here we encountered dense fog that reduced visibility to near zero. This is common for the area, but my ten-year-old brain was telling me that we were going to drive off the side of the road into the abyss and never be heard from again. Fear not, all ended well. We made it to Hungary for Christmas and back to Milan for our flight home.

The last memory I have from this trip was an unfortunate incident at the Milan airport. I was waiting for my dad when a lady sitting near me walked away, leaving her duty-free bag on the seat. Before I could do anything, a man working at a nearby bar sprinted out and grabbed it. Within minutes the lady came rushing back and up to the bartender, presumably asking if anyone had turned in her bag. Shoulders shrugging, hands elevated, his body language said it all. She left empty-handed. I was stunned but sat there speechless. I didn't have the courage to speak up at the time, but I think the experience may have helped me recognise that I do have a voice.

Perhaps that is why a little story I read years later also stuck with me. It was about a young boy picking up stranded starfish along a beach and, one at a time, throwing them back into the ocean. A stranger came along and asked what he was doing. 'I'm throwing starfish back into the water to save them,' the boy responded. 'There are too many.' The stranger countered, 'You are never going to make a difference.' The boy calmly picked up another starfish, threw it back into the water and replied, 'Made a difference to that one!'

After those experiences as a ten-year-old you might think I would have been turned off Italy. But not so. The people intrigued me, as did the language, the stand-up coffee bars, and everything else I soaked up during that short visit. Even at that young age I was prepared to keep an open mind. I also sensed there was a lot more out there worth exploring.

CHAPTER 4

Dal Mare alle Montagne –
From Sea to Mountains

Men go abroad to wonder at the heights of the mountains,
at the huge waves of the sea, at the long courses of the rivers,
at the vast compass of the ocean, at the circular motions of
the stars, and they pass by themselves without wondering.
                                          —St Augustine

For a country of around 60 million people (less than one percent of the world's population), Italy has an immensely rich historical, cultural, and artistic heritage. Think Dante and Botticelli, Michelangelo and Leonardo, Galileo and Columbus, Puccini and Verdi, to name a few in a long list. It is also the country that, with China, is home to the greatest number of UNESCO World Heritage sites. The following brief synopsis provides some context for the stories and experiences you will read about, and a basic understanding of the lay of the land.

History

Italy as we know it today was built over thousands of drama-filled years. The Romans dominated for almost ten centuries, but both before and after the Romans the peninsula suffered under a myriad of invading armies and marauders that laid claim to various portions of it.

The age of the Romans—first the Republic and then the Empire—lasted from about 500 BC to 500 AD. The early period of the Republic was focused on building Rome into a world power by systematically conquering the Mediterranean area and substantial portions of Europe. The Republic functioned effectively until civil war broke out in 49 BC, precipitated by Julius Caesar when he famously 'crossed the Rubicon', the river boundary between the Roman province of Gaul to the north and Italy proper. This ultimately led to his assassination and formation of the Roman Empire under Emperor Augustus.

Imperial rule survived under a series of Emperors until the fifth century AD, but this later period was characterised by civil unrest, the break-up of the Empire into East (Byzantium) and West (Rome), and an onset of barbarian invasions. After the western portion of the Empire fell in 476, the region broke up into smaller bodies. The Papal States, independent territories governed by the Catholic Pope, were established in 754; and powerful city-states, including Florence, Venice, and Genoa, also emerged at this time. As these cities grew in wealth and prestige through trade and commerce, they also became important centres of art and learning, fostering the Renaissance (c1300–1600).

In succeeding centuries Italy continued to suffer invasions by various European powers, such as France, Austria, and Spain, which spurred the growth of independence movements and calls for unification. The *Risorgimento,* or Italian unification movement, consisted of a chain of political and military events that culminated in the establishment of the Kingdom of Italy in 1861 under Victor Emmanuel II, the first king of Italy. Victor Emmanuel is celebrated as one of the four 'fathers of the fatherland' for his role in uniting the country, along with Giuseppe Garibaldi, Giuseppe Mazzini, and Count Cavour. You will not go anywhere in Italy that does not have streets, piazzas, and monuments honouring these Italian heroes. A national monument to the king's memory, an impressive white marble edifice called the Altare della Patria (Altar of the Fatherland), can be found between Piazza Venezia and Capitoline Hill in the heart of Rome. With its location at the hub of ancient Rome (the four major roads of Rome converge in Piazza Venezia), the Piazza embraces the modern city and is symbolic of a free and united Italy.

Despite being on the winning side in World War I, Italian nationalists remained unhappy as social and economic difficulties continued to plague the country. This discontent paved the way for fascism and the rise of Benito Mussolini, who swept into power in 1922. The fascist leader turned the office of President into a dictatorship and allied with Germany under Hitler in World War II.

A shepherd in Campo Imperatore.

I was introduced to a little history about Mussolini on a visit to Campo Imperatore (Emperor's Field) in the mountainous Abruzzo region, famous for its national parks and nature reserves. The hotel at the alpine ski resort (one of Italy's oldest) was Mussolini's short-lived prison in 1943 in the wake of his fall from power. The area is a vast alpine meadow in a basin-shaped plateau in Gran Sasso National Park. The bleak surroundings and high altitude seemed to offer a secure location, but it did not withstand a dramatic escape orchestrated by the Germans. Photographs and Mussolini memorabilia from that era are still on display in the hotel.

After years of fierce fighting, Italy was liberated from German occupation in 1945, the same year Mussolini was executed. Democracy was reinstated following World War II and the existing monarchy abolished in favour of a republic, but much unrest remained. Various coalition governments were unable to provide stability amidst the flaring Cold War rivalry between the United States and the Soviet Union. However, because of its strategic significance, the US provided Italy with generous financial assistance through the Marshall Plan (European Recovery Program), helping to carry it forward. A growing demand for metal and other manufactured goods further stimulated Italy's economy. The growth continued until the late 1960s, but between 1958 and 1963, in particular, Italy experienced a prolonged period of economic growth, dubbed the 'economic miracle', which transformed it from a mainly poor, rural nation into a global industrial powerhouse.

Modern Italy

Modern Italy is made up of twenty politically autonomous regions, their borders corresponding loosely to those that existed prior to unification. Five regions were given special status and greater independence in recognition of their cultural and linguistic diversity. These regions are Aosta Valley, Trentino-Alto Adige, Friuli Venezia Giulia, and the island regions of Sardinia and Sicily. Other than Italy's smallest region, Aosta Valley, each is divided into various provinces.

While mentioning the number of regions in Italy, I am certain my friend Giovanni won't mind if I share a funny story. When I was staying at his B&B in Chianti, our host referred to Italy's twenty-four regions. *Scusa?* I knew beyond doubt there are only twenty—I have spent too many years figuring out how to get to all of them. I politely suggested he check his facts, and happily Italy continues to be composed of twenty regions. We both had a good laugh.

Geography

Italy is not a large country. The boot-shaped peninsula is about the size of Arizona, or half the size of my home province of Alberta. If you land at Rome's international airport on the west coast, you can be clear across the country to the Adriatic Sea in well under three hours, even with a mountain range in between. Or, if so inclined, you could have breakfast in Milan, close to Italy's northern border with Switzerland, and get to Reggio di Calabria in the southern region of Calabria in time for a late dinner, maybe even earlier if you drive *come un Italiano.* So, despite Italy having twenty regions, if for some unfortunate reason you must, you could cover quite a bit of that territory in relatively short order.

When my husband and I recently drove from southern California to our home in Alberta, I amused myself by comparing distances. We drove over 2,700 km in two long days on that trip, equivalent to driving from Italy's southern tip to its northern border—and almost all the way back again the next day. We just wanted to get home safely during the outbreak of the COVID-19 pandemic, but when I look at it from an Italian perspective it does seem a little *pazzo*.

I know the notion of covering these distances in one day is something many older Italians simply don't comprehend. I have met an Italian who has lived his entire life within a 100 km radius of where he was born. I'm thinking of Antonio, aged 78 when I first met him in northern Lazio. He'd been to Rome for his honeymoon, just over 100 km away, but otherwise had never been any further from his hometown of Cellere. I also met a *nonna* walking her grandson in the small town of Cella Monte (Piedmont). Since moving to northern Italy from Calabria following her marriage, she had never been back, despite still having family there. It was difficult to wrap my brain around these anecdotes, but as I learned more about Italy's history and culture, I began to understand how profoundly different the lives of many Italian elderly are from my own.

The Italian peninsula extends from the European Alps in a southeasterly direction into the Mediterranean Sea. To the north of Italy lie Switzerland and Austria, to the east Slovenia and the Adriatic Sea, to the west France and the Ligurian and Tyrrhenian seas, and to the south the Ionian and Mediterranean seas. In addition to the Republic of Italy, two other independent countries exist within its boundaries: Vatican City (a city-state) and the Republic of San Marino. While I write this, my Italian language classes come to mind. At exam time we'd have to memorise facts such as the names and *capoluoghi* (regional capitals) of all twenty regions, the volcanoes, longest river, highest mountain, and the five seas surrounding Italy. We also had to know the three countries within the Italian peninsula. So now you know too! It sounds like a geography class, rather than Italian, but it was Antonella's way of teaching us about Italy as she taught us its language. It was all part of the attraction for me. As a bonus, I could impress my Italian friends by rhyming off all twenty regions and each capital city.

Almost forty percent of Italy is mountainous. Its northern border is fringed by the Alps, and the Apennine Mountains run southeast through the peninsula, like a backbone. The UNESCO-designated Dolomites are part of the southern Alps, taking their name from French geologist Déodat de Dolomieu who discovered the unique properties of the hard, chalky rock composed of calcium and magnesium. The composition of the rocks creates the world-famous 'alpenglow' effect that turns the mountains wonderful shades of pale pink and purple, even fiery red, at dawn and dusk. Sitting in her cabin in the mountain town of Sappada (Friuli Venezia Giulia), a friend's mother pointed out this phenomenon from her window, noting that it is what she loved most about being there.

Where there are mountains there are also rivers and lakes. The Po River, Italy's longest, flows across northern Italy from the southwestern Alps to the Adriatic Sea. The fertile Po Valley represents over seventy percent of Italy's total plains area, making it a virtual breadbasket for the country. The Adige River, Italy's second longest, has its headwaters in the Alps, near the Austrian border, and makes its way across northern Italy to the Adriatic Sea. The historic Tiber, which begins its journey in the mountains of Umbria and Lazio, flows through Rome and west to the Tyrrhenian Sea. Further north, the Arno River flows west through Florence and out to the Ligurian Sea. Italy is also home to several large lakes, including Lake Como, Lake Garda, and Lake Maggiore, just a few of Italy's many picturesque lakes located in the Lake District.

Italy's largest islands include Elba (Tuscany) and the autonomous regions of Sicily and Sardinia. Smaller islands and archipelagos dot the Italian coastline, many of them volcanic.

Italy is also famous for its numerous volcanoes, including some that are still active, such as Etna, Vulcano, and Stromboli in Sicily, and Vesuvius south of Naples.

Italy cannot be defined by its geography and history. But at the same time, Italy would not be the country it is today without them.

CHAPTER 5

La Bella Lingua –
The Beautiful Language

A different language is a different vision of life.
—Federico Fellini

I laughed when I came across someone calling himself the Dolomites Mountain Guide who said, 'Many think Italians are one generic people: spaghetti-eating, Vespa-riding (with a minimum of three per machine!), mandolin-playing members of the Mafia. Wrong!' With an intimate knowledge of local history, the writer went on to explain that Italians are a mix of many different ethnic groups 'with different languages, different traditions, different ways of thinking . . . all gathered together in a small country'. In the Dolomites region alone, for example, you will find three main ethnic groups, each with their own dialects. In some valleys German is spoken, in others Italian is the main language, and along the Adige valley between Trento and Bolzano both are used.

I understood exactly what he was talking about based on an earlier visit to the northern region of Trentino-Alto Adige, where I found the German influence overtly noticeable. Stopping for lunch in the city of Bolzano (where the Dolomites Mountain Guide, Roberto, happens to be from), it had surprised me that German was the first language on the menu. Many food selections also had a decidedly German flair, such as *speck* (cured pork using German curing techniques), *canederli* (bread dumplings), polenta with beef goulash, and strudel.

The experience was similar along the eastern and northern shores of nearby Lake Garda. I learned that this area is referred to as Italy's Northern Riviera by Germans and Austrians who flock here from across the Alps, attracted by milder temperatures and easy access. In Riva del Garda, a popular tourist location and mecca for outdoor sports enthusiasts perched on the northern tip of the lake, I had an even more unexpected experience. As I entered a store, the owner greeted me in German. Hearing no immediate response, he then asked, 'German? Swedish?' *Canadese*, I responded. 'Ah, Canada! Ah, Beautiful!' His confusion can be easily forgiven. I was a tall blonde in an area saturated with Germans. His language of choice also reflects the region's history.

Formerly part of the Austro-Hungarian Empire, the area has experienced a history of shifting borders. For example, the German-speaking province of Alto Adige was part of the South Tyrol region of Austria until it was ceded to Italy following World War I. Tensions persisted until the end of World War II, when Italy and Austria eventually negotiated an agreement that recognised both Italian and German as official languages of the region. The German-speaking population was also granted a significant level of self-governance to help settle ongoing ethnic disputes. The result is a sense that you are in two different worlds when moving between the two provinces of this region. While places evolve with time, many South Tyrol residents with Austrian ancestry choose to maintain their linguistic and cultural uniqueness and cling to their traditions. As magnificent as it was, the location was not ideal for someone hoping to speak Italian and eat more conventional Italian food.

The evolution of Italy's national language is similarly complex. What has come to be known today as standard Italian is a direct descendent of the Tuscan dialect, the language of the Florentine poet Dante Alighieri. His poems were widely read throughout Tuscany and beyond, but his epic work, *The Divine Comedy*, was not translated. Nonetheless, viewing one's ability to read Dante's original text as a sign of educational status, the upper classes across Italy chose to read his work in the Tuscan dialect. Over time, Tuscan became the most widely understood dialect throughout Italy so that, in effect, Italy had a national language many centuries before it was a country itself.

When Italy was finally unified in 1861, the Tuscan dialect was adopted as the official language even though only a small percentage of Italians could speak it. That percentage continues to rise as standard Italian is taught in schools and as elderly speakers of regional dialects die, but still it is not universally spoken. The slow uptake can in large part be attributed to the many groups who continue to rely on a mosaic of regional languages. These are often referred to as dialects, although technically they are separate languages since they are not descendants or variants of official Italian.

Even as standard Italian has spread throughout Italy, regional varieties have also developed. Language variation, reflecting small changes between different groups of speakers, commonly occurs on a continuum throughout a region, sometimes even locally. As an example, although the villages of Cinque Terre (Liguria) span less than 25 km, there are small peculiarities in speech that allow locals to tell which village a person is from. The explanation likely relates to limited travel in the old days, as well as the relative inaccessibility of these remote villages.

The regional varieties of standard Italian should not be confused with indigenous languages that predate the national language. Twelve such languages have been officially recognised as 'linguistic minorities', the largest being Sardu. Like Sardinia itself, Sardu is a mix of various influences stemming from the political history of the island, including Byzantine Greek, Catalan, Spanish, and Italian. Quite different than other Romance languages, it apparently has no connection to any dialects of mainland Italy and is virtually incomprehensible even to other Italians. Luckily for me, my Sardinian friend Rosanna speaks Italian as well as Sardu.

The historic underdevelopment of southern Italy, in contrast to the more prosperous North, has been an ongoing challenge. The differences between the *Mezzogiorno* (a term for the regions south of Rome plus Sicily and Sardinia) and the rest of Italy can be staggering. Some even see Italy as two nations because of the stark disparity between North and South. These discrepancies extend beyond an economy where the South's per capita income is significantly below that of central and northern Italy, to social and cultural aspects as well.

The extreme poverty of the rural South was historically the driving force behind emigration from southern regions of the Italian peninsula, and from Sicily. Unlike the more prosperous and educated North, at the time of unification southern Italy had seen little economic advancement. The population was largely poor and uneducated, held back by factors such as a lack of roads and ports, rural overpopulation, and outdated agricultural practices. The first mass diaspora began in the 1880s and saw millions from southern Italy flood across the Atlantic to North and South America, including Canada, the United States, Brazil, and Argentina. A second mass exodus continued after World War II up to the 1970s, when many more left Italy out of necessity, in search of a better life.

Most Italian immigrants to North America came from southern regions, including Campania, Basilicata, Calabria, and Sicily. This demographic helps explain why we often hear regional variations spoken by Italian immigrants. They brought their dialects with them, many never having learned formal Italian, and many elderly Italians never learning much English after they arrived. The first-generation Italian Canadians I met playing soccer often learned their 'Italian' from their parents and grandparents. As a result, they often knew only the dialect of the region their family migrated from. Of course, there are many exceptions, and more recently, younger Italians have been emigrating from Italy looking for better futures and career opportunities. I know two young, educated couples who came to Canada from northern Italy exactly for this reason. All speak standard Italian, and their local dialect, and now English as well. They have become friends and I have had the privilege of learning more about Italy through their eyes.

We also have Sicilian friends who migrated to Canada in their youth. Sicilian is another officially recognised minority language, and the differences are striking. As with Sardu, it is nothing like the language I've been learning, but it is part of Italy's colourful history that adds to my fascination. And, as people seem inclined to do, the first word one Sicilian friend taught me was one I can assure you is not in my phrase books. Technically referring to the male reproductive organ, *minchia* is a southern variation of *cazzo* (dick). While it can be considered rude depending on the circumstance, these words are commonly thrown around in day-to-day conversations, even by women. Another friend's elderly mother once exclaimed *Cap d' stu cazz'* (literally 'head of the dick') simply because her coffee didn't have sugar in it, as she liked. While this is an expression particular to Fondi, you get the idea.

The first time I can remember noting some pronunciation that was distinctive to Tuscany was when I joined my B&B hosts on their sailboat for a weekend excursion to Elba Island. Among the guests were a couple from outside Florence, the regional capital of Tuscany. I learned that the strange sound

I was hearing is referred to as an 'aspirated c', one of the most distinguishing features of Tuscan pronunciation. For example, instead of saying 'coca cola' with a hard 'c' (sounding like koka kola in the rest of Italy), in Tuscany you would hear *hoka hola*. Sorry Luca, but it was hard not to laugh when you talked about buying *hoka hola* at the *hentro hommerciale!*

Dialects aside, I always took pride in locals telling me, *Parli bene* (You speak well). It made me feel more connected when they understood me and appreciated my efforts. I have been super lucky to have strong Italian teachers to help me with my pronunciation, as well as good friend Joe F, a retired high school teacher. I laugh recalling how Joe would joke, 'You have to put the acc**en**te on the right sill**ab**le', while emphasising the wrong syllables himself.

One of my fondest memories regarding my Italian relates to an email exchange I had as we were making our way down the Adriatic coast, through the regions of Marche and Abruzzo. Using my mobile device, I wrote in Italian to the family-run hotel where we had reservations, asking for directions. I was shocked to get a detailed response, also in Italian, including numerous words I didn't know. What had I set myself up for? The context helped me figure them out, fortunately, and we arrived without difficulty. When Gord stopped by the front desk the next morning to check out, the girl apologised for not having written back in English. She had assumed I spoke Italian based on my email. Wow! That made my day. I find it easier to read and write than to find the words to speak myself. However, with my combination of classes and opportunities to spend time in Italy, it is slowly coming together. And when I feel like I'm losing a step, that is my excuse for heading back to Italy—*Ho bisogno di practicare il mio italiano* (I need to practice my Italian).

Especially in the early days, I was constantly looking for ways to practise my Italian. In addition to asking for directions, always a good conversation starter, elderly men became my best friends. Wherever I looked, conversations were there to be found; they were always willing to chat. As another strategy, I might ask if I could take a picture, and a discussion would ensue. From an early encounter in the Tuscan hilltop town of San Gimignano, I learned to ask if I could *fare una foto* ('do' or 'make' a picture) rather than the Italian equivalent of 'take' a picture. In return, one of the *anziani* (elderly) asked in Italian where I was taking it. In other words, where was I from. It put a smile on his face when I said that he was going to be famous in Canada!

On another occasion, a group of men sitting in a shady archway of a stone wall in the Etruscan town of Tarquinia (Lazio) seemed like a perfect audience. While my friends hung back and watched with amusement, I approached and asked if I could take their picture. At that point, all hell seemed to break loose. Clearly these seniors were lifelong friends, and with their fair share of spunk. They started poking fun at one of their friends, with the whole group laughing. I learned that they were debating who was the best looking.

A similar experience took place more recently on Elba Island, the biggest in the Tuscany Archipelago. I went for a morning walk around the small marina in Porto Azzurro and noticed six men crowded onto one bench. On my return they were still huddled along the bench. Slightly amused, I stopped to ask if I could take a picture. They consented, although I don't recall getting a smile out of any of them. When I asked if they'd like copies of the photo, not one had an email address—not totally surprising given their age. So, I did it the old-fashioned way. I took the postal address of one gentleman and agreed to mail the photos. Back home in Canada I made six copies and sent them along as promised. Without any further contact I could never be certain the men received their photographs, but at least I know where to find them.

A group of friends sitting together in Porto Azzurro.

I was in my element when these opportunities arose. And while I can pretty much guarantee that I would not be asking strangers at home if I could take their picture, in Italy it felt acceptable. In addition to appreciating the interaction with locals, I loved the picture-taking process itself. I enjoyed setting up each shot, figuring out where the best light would be, how to frame it to be more visually appealing. At times it felt like I was learning about Italy and its people through the lens of my camera.

I read that when you learn a new language it changes who you are. I am by no means fluent, but I'm inclined to agree. When I speak or read in Italian, I reflect on things differently. I look for ways to express myself, not only to be understood but also to fit in. I have always talked with my hands, so that is nothing new, but the rather boring monotone voice I seem to have much of the time becomes more expressive and energetic.

I'm comfortable rolling my r's and articulating each syllable. I feel like my personality changes as well.

And there is research to back me up—people who speak different languages do indeed think differently. When you are learning a new language, you are not simply learning a new way of talking, you are also inadvertently learning a new way of thinking. This notion also had me thinking of a quote I read by the inspirational author, Wayne Dyer: 'Change the way you look at things and the things you look at change.'

CHAPTER 6

Chiedere Aiuto – Asking for Help

Not all who wander are lost.
—J.R.R. Tolken

I took my initial Italian language class in preparation for our first major trip to Italy, and with that to my credit I became our group's unofficial tour guide. This was before the now prolific use of mobile devices—back when we were still using compasses and the North Star to find our way. If you've driven in Italy, I know I'm preaching to the converted when I say it is not easy. Arrows that look like they are directing you to the left, for example, in fact are telling you to go straight. And at traffic circles there can be four or five exits, or even double circles, and only seconds to figure out which exit you are supposed to take, before you miss it. And we certainly had our share of misses!

When we were unsure which way to turn, if not hopelessly lost, I would get out, approach a passer-by with *Mi scusi*, and use my limited Italian to try and get us back on track. I could usually take in the first instruction or two, but the rest often came out in double time and was hopelessly lost on me. Inevitably we would have to pull over again and I'd pick up the conversation with someone new. A positive aspect was that my Italian was improving. Many words became much easier to recall in context, and I learned new words every time we stopped.

A little aside. When my sister and I were biking in France years ago, we would find ourselves in similar situations. We knew some French from school, but when a local told us to go 'tout droit' and signalled straight ahead, we were totally confused. We didn't realise that this expression meant to continue in the same direction. What we heard was 'droit', as in '(turn) right'. Not surprisingly, it wasn't long before we were stopping again. I didn't figure this expression out until years later when I began studying Italian. *Sempre dritto* in Italian literally means 'always straight' but somehow it clicked with me that 'tout droit' in French (everything right) meant the same thing—just keep on going.

A trick we used when driving into a city was to follow the black and white 'bull's-eye' signs, as we liked to call them, indicating *il centro*. In the medieval hilltop towns of Tuscany, for example, this usually guaranteed arrival outside the protective ramparts of the historic centre. We would park near the stone walls and head through the massive arched entrances and along the narrow streets until we found the heart of the town, its main piazza.

They say first impressions matter, and we certainly fell in love with Bologna, capital of Emilia-Romagna, for that reason. We got off to a bad start by inadvertently driving into the city centre, which requires a special permit. Then, to make the situation worse, or so we thought, we immediately saw a police vehicle on the roadside—*carabinieri* in this case, the national police force with a local arm in every town. We decided to stop for directions, thinking we could play dumb *turisti* if necessary. Instead, they led us to a nearby garage where we could park without a permit. In other words, no ticket. The garage attendant was also kind, giving us directions to the centre and for getting out of town later. A third kind incident happened when we stopped for cold water and discovered we didn't have enough small change. We were going to leave empty-handed, but a young attendant motioned for us to just take the bottle. Another nice surprise.

Bologna was also captivating for other reasons. Despite significant damage during World War II, the city has one of the largest medieval centres in Italy, containing many streets lined with attractive arcades, or porticos, of which we walked a few. The vibrant atmosphere, in part thanks to students attending the oldest university in Europe (opened in 1088), was also attractive. And when I found out that it is known as a haven for foodies, I quickly added Bologna to my list of places to revisit.

You never know what you're going to get when asking for help. That was the case when I asked a little girl in the port city of Bari (Apulia) if we were heading in the right direction for Basilica di San Nicola. Bari's old town (*Barivecchia*) was making directions a challenge. The girl responded in Italian, and when I said *Grazie*, to thank her, her response was 'For nothing'. With enough Italian in my back pocket, I knew this was a rather literal translation of *di niente*, one way an Italian would say 'You're welcome'. *Che carina!* How cute.

One of the funniest responses I got was in Campobasso, the capital of Molise, a small mountainous region in southern Italy that until 1963 was part of neighbouring Abruzzo. Faced with a series of confusing lanes and stairways as we climbed up to Castello Monforte, I stopped to check our route with an elderly lady leaning out her window. She waved her hand in the direction we were heading and said *Sopra. Sempre Sopra.* The literal translation means 'always above' but what she was telling us was to 'keep on climbing'. We made it in time to explore the roofless castle, check out views of the green valleys below, and enjoy one of my favourite pastimes, watching the golden sun as it set over the Apennine Mountains to the west. We also found a more user-friendly route down, along the Salita dei Monti

(Ascent of the Mountains), for which I was thankful as the light faded.

While staying at an agriturismo in the southeastern region of Apulia, I was offered a little more than I bargained for. On a free afternoon I decided to take advantage of an available bicycle to go exploring. Before long I coasted into a small centre called Soleto. As I rode through this rather nondescript town, I passed a bench occupied by two men. No surprise there. I offered a *Ciao!* and a wave as I glided by and got a cordial *Ciao!* back. Having second thoughts, I circled back, wondering what there might be to see in this sleepy town. Speaking absolutely no English, one of the men offered to show me the churches.

Normally I would have respectfully declined, but right or wrong I opted in. I didn't feel threatened in any way—it was broad daylight and I had approached the man versus him approaching me. And it was just more appealing to have a local guide. Unfortunately, it proved to be a short tour with little to show for my time. In addition to having no unique attractions, the churches were closed. After my new friend shared a few details about his hometown's history, I extended my hand to say 'good-bye'. To my amusement more than anything, my new pal was hoping for a kiss goodbye. Like a kiss-kiss! After a little good-humoured negotiating he settled for a selfie as he gave me a peck on the cheek. *Solo in Italia.* Only in Italy.

On several occasions I stayed at Gatta Morena, a B&B in a rural area of Lazio. Antonio, who I've mentioned previously, lived in town but had a garden nearby. One morning, as was his custom, he stopped by the B&B for coffee with Elio. I was planning to hike into the village of Cellere, known for its well-preserved Renaissance church Sant'Egidio Abate, so took the opportunity to ask for directions. Even though it was less than an hour on foot, and we could see the village from where we were sitting, do you think they could agree on a route? Eventually I headed off with a hand-drawn map Elio had scratched on a scrap of paper. More memorable was when I got to an intersection where I was supposed to turn. Antonio was sitting in his little car waiting for me, 'Just to be sure,' he said in Italian.

You will hear more about the Gatta Morena friends who had a major impact on my impressions of Italy, and on me. But with that incident in mind, here is some advice from the Dolomites Mountain Guide: 'Once you are in Italy, always ask locals for information. Local knowledge is an important asset. Ask the same question of at least two people and compare the answers. If the answers are different, ask a third person.' Very astute!

We could really have used some local help en route from Venice to Bolzano. We ended up on a slower 'blue road' north of Venice and kept seeing the autostrada in various spots but could never figure out where to get on it. Thankfully, we didn't have to learn another simple autostrada lesson the hard way. With the high speeds that some people prefer to drive on these already fast roads, you absolutely must stay to the right. In North America it is not uncommon for drivers on a three-lane highway to pass cars on either side, but this is unheard of in Italy. You stay right and move to your left to pass slower cars. Period. End of discussion. If you're foolish enough to remain in the left-hand lane, you will have some fancy car up your butt before you can say gelato.

Speaking of gelato, a friend has a funny colloquial expression he likes to pull out when anyone mentions gelato—*È meglio un culo gelato che un gelato in culo.* In other words, it is better to have a cold behind (a nicer word for culo), than to have ice cream up your culo. I'm quite sure he's right. Travel is never all peaches and gelato though, so I think it's important to talk about the good, the bad, and the ugly! While it doesn't necessarily feel like it at the time, the latter is where the biggest lessons are often found.

Trying to find the train station in Florence on a visit with friends was unfortunately in the ugly category. Between the three of us (me as a back-seat driver likely being more of a hindrance than a help) and the not so helpful road map we were using back then, we must have spent an hour driving around the city trying to find Santa Maria Novella railway station. Our first error was missing our exit, which took us to the opposite side of town, and things went downhill from there. In our defence, the centre of Florence is a driver's nightmare, with its one-way streets and, like Bologna, an electronically controlled historic centre. No surprise, we got a ticket for being in the restricted area without a permit. In true Italian style, it didn't arrive in Canada for at least six months.

Regrettably, this was not the only time Florence messed me up, or more aptly, I messed up in Florence. On an earlier visit I had an even uglier experience. We had rented an apartment in the old centre that included parking, but do you think we could get to it? I even got out of our car at one point, ran around the corner and stood right in front of our apartment. But that road was a one-way, going the other direction of course. I should have tried to find the apartment owner, but our car was sitting in the middle of a busy street, so I jumped back in. It took more driving around in an emotional daze to finally get back to the apartment with our vehicle, which we did out of sheer luck more than anything. To make matters worse, there was absolutely no way we were going to get our car through the narrow gate, off an even narrower street, with unforgiving stone walls surrounding us.

I confess to having a serious meltdown before it was all said and done, one that thankfully I have yet to top. We did not get to see much of Florence that day. However, after we met our host, had a glass or two of vino, and settled down (speaking for myself here), we did venture out to find the restaurant he recommended. It was a short walk over the Arno River, across the historic Ponte Vecchio (Old Bridge) no less, and we relaxed into our chairs. As we struck up a conversation with the couple next to us who were speaking English, it was exiting to discover that one was the doctor of a famous golfer from Argentina who, as it happened, had just won the US Open. I'm sure any golfers out there will know who I'm talking about.

Eventually we had another opportunity to return to Florence and happily this time it was a charm. Third time lucky! We wandered around with our traveling companions and took in the sights like real tourists.

Florence, looking at the Ponte Vecchio and the Arno River.

In Ravenna (Emilia-Romagna) with my mom and sister, we managed to get ourselves utterly turned around trying to find its famous Byzantine mosaics. I'm not sure what our problem was, but it was a frustrating experience all round. We eventually got ourselves on track with the aid of a passer-by, found a place to park, and made our way to the Basilica of San Vitale (548 AD). Among the most important monuments of early Christian art in Italy, San Vitale is famous for its splendid mosaics. Beside the Basilica is the Mausoleum of Galla Placidia (c425 AD), its unassuming exterior in stark contrast to the vibrant mosaics decorating the upper part of the building, including the captivating starry sky mosaic of the cupola. For the 'universal value and uniqueness' of their mosaics, these and other early Christian religious monuments in Ravenna were added to UNESCO's World Heritage List in 1996. I know my mother was more interested in the religious symbolism and stories the mosaics told, but I recall being amazed that such magnificent pictures could be created out of so many tiny pieces of coloured glass.

I was offered some unexpected help when asking for assistance in the little hilltop town of Monte San Biagio (Lazio). We were meandering around the old town and saw a sign for the castle. You would think something that size would be easy to spot, but the narrow streets made it a challenge. Mysteriously, the castle signs had also disappeared. I stopped to check with locals we found chatting in a tiny piazza, and it was our lucky day. One of the men told us the castle was closed, but then followed up with an offer to let us in. He was keeper of the keys, apparently. After escorting us through a gate, he motioned for us to climb to the top of the *torre* on our own. We were rewarded with a view extending over Lago di Fondi and out to the Tyrrhenian Sea. *Grazie Signore.*

In Merano (Trentino-Alto Adige) we came across parking spaces thoughtfully reserved for 'Women Only'. They were designed specifically to be wider than the other spaces. There evidently is some logic to this offering. It is a generality, but I did read that women statistically have more issues with spatial awareness than men. I was not offended, though, thinking that the dings on my car might support this hypothesis. It was encouraging to know that I could blame something other than my poor driving skills.

With friends one summer, I had a different challenge in a parking lot. After our driver (let's call her Ms. Daisy, to protect the guilty) parked the car, we headed into a store. As we came out, we were greeted by a street vendor pointing at our vehicle. It was parked quite oddly, on an angle across two spaces. With his help, though he didn't seem to speak Italian or English, we began to piece things together. Ms. Daisy had managed to leave the car in gear, and it had started to move after our backs were turned. The vendor had tried to attract our attention, but we ignored him, assuming he was trying to entice us to buy something. We even heard an announcement inside that included a licence plate number, but it didn't register. Thankfully, there were no cars parked nearby, and our runaway had stopped on its own before doing any damage. We did have a good laugh and apologized to the vendor.

We had another little incident in Rome, this time with Ms. Daisy's suitcases, which had us all laughing again. It was her first trip to Europe, so understandably difficult to know what to pack. But she must have brought half her wardrobe—you know, just in case. Packing is one of those things many of us unfortunately need to learn the hard way. Her clothes were neatly stacked, but there was just so much stuff. I'm guessing she never even remembered most of what she had with her, and certainly did not come close to wearing it all.

With that in mind, picture Ms. Daisy lugging an extra-large suitcase, plus her carry-on, on and off the train into Rome, including up and down stairs under the railway tracks. Getting the picture? While boarding the train at Civitavecchia (Rome's port of call), the three of us who climbed on first loaded our cases overhead, took our seats, and then watched in disbelief as Ms. Daisy tried to muscle her oversized suitcase through an unforgiving doorway. A male passenger beside us said something along the lines of 'This looks like a scene from *Sex in the City*.' We glanced at each other with wide eyes. I wasn't exactly sure what he meant but was quite sure it was not a compliment.

But wait, there's more! If you're familiar with Italian train stations you will know that, depending which *binario* (track or platform) you arrive at, you may need to go down a steep set of stairs, through a tunnel, and back up the other side. This was the situation when we arrived at Rome's San Pietro Station, close to the apartment we had rented. So here was Ms. Daisy, dragging her suitcase and carry-on down the stairs, bumpety, bumpety, bump. Noise aside, she managed to get to the bottom with wheels intact. From there we had a long flight of stairs up the other side. Any of us would have helped, but we had our own bags to contend with. While Ms. Daisy was taking a break, a priest who was witnessing this debacle swept in from behind and, without a word, carried her big suitcase up the remaining stairs. He was quite small and fully robed, hardly the image of a knight in shining armour, which made the whole thing even more comical. All we could say was *Grazie Padre* and count our blessings.

This chapter would not be complete without a note about technology. Although I'd been making annual treks to Italy for quite a few years, it wasn't until 2012 that I dragged myself into the twenty-first century in terms of the technology I was using. While walking back to our car in Bologna, we spotted an electronics store and decided to check out our options. I ended up purchasing a local SIM card and a reasonably priced one-month phone package. Why I didn't consider this option earlier is beyond me, but it certainly made our lives a lot easier going forward. At least most of the time.

I've had my share of frustrating moments with technology for sure, such as accidently purchasing a SIM card for a phone instead of an iPad or purchasing a SIM card and coverage at Malpensa airport in Milan (for an obscene amount I might add) that did not activate until two days later. Not overly helpful when I had purchased it specifically to help with driving directions. We've since made friends at a local telecom store in Fondi, our Italian home away from home. It's a perfect relationship—I practise my Italian and he takes care of our mobile devices.

CHAPTER 7

Il Cuore della Città –
The Heart of the City

For me a town is not judged by its museums and masterpieces, but by its piazza.

—Christine Webb

While they may be called agora, forum, piazza, plaza, platz, marketplace, or any number of other names, the main square has been a distinguishing characteristic of cities across Europe for well over two thousand years. During early Roman rule, piazzas were created at the intersection of the main roads through town and revered as sacred ground. This public space was traditionally flanked by a temple and a civic forum. More elaborate squares would perhaps include a central marketplace and shops fronted by colonnades and tenements above.

A well-known example from this era is Piazza della Rotonda in Rome, which offers visitors a splendid view of the Pantheon, a Roman temple built during the reign of Emperor Hadrian (125 AD). The Romans borrowed heavily from the Greeks when developing their own style of architecture, but it was their invention of concrete that enabled the construction of arches, vaults, and domes. The Pantheon remains one of Rome's best-preserved ancient buildings, its dome still the largest unreinforced concrete dome in the world. While the Pantheon itself would certainly be on the radar of most tourists, everyone should also take time to appreciate 'life in the piazza'. A central fountain provides a soothing place to linger, while surrounding restaurants and cafes add vibrancy well into the evening.

Other piazzas dating from Roman times and beyond vary considerably in shape and size, depending in part on their origins. Piazza Mercato in the Tuscan town of Lucca, for example, is oval, having been built on the foundations of a Roman amphitheatre. Lucca is also famous for its massive ramparts. Originally built to protect the town, the ancient walls are now enjoyed as a public space where citizens and visitors alike, myself included, can stroll, jog, or cycle atop the wide walls.

And in Rome's oval-shaped Piazza Navona, home of Bernini's iconic Fontana Dei Quattro Fiumi (Fountain of the Four Rivers), surrounding edifices were built on the ruined grandstands of a first-century Roman stadium (Stadio di Domiziano). The space was home to a city market for hundreds of years until the market was moved to a nearby piazza called Campo de' Fiori (meaning 'Field of Flowers', which it once was) in 1869. Today visitors flock to Piazza Navona to take in its historical landmarks, or to shop or relax at its cafes and restaurants and enjoy the street artists who add colour and flair. I decided to use the Fountain of the Four Rivers as a meeting place once, and as it turned out I was not the only one with this brilliant idea—it's the most popular meeting place in Rome, I later learned.

After the Roman Empire collapsed, political power, trade, and commerce in Italy came to be centred on the independent city-states that grew in power and prestige during the Middle Ages. A feature of medieval towns and cities was their central marketplace or town square, which helped to foster a strong sense of community and culture. It was during this period that Siena's Piazza del Campo, known locally as *Il Campo*, was created. Edged by ornate buildings such as the thirteenth-century

Gothic Palazzo Pubblico, and humming restaurants and cafes, this pedestrian-only space is a hub of everyday life in Siena—its sloped bowl shape creating a natural amphitheatre and a visual sense of enclosure.

The famous Siena Palio also takes place here twice a year. The event's focus is a bareback horse race, with the colours of the *contrade*, or districts of the city, flying wildly as riders make several loops around the Piazza. Citizens of the victorious *contrada* erupt into celebrations and are rewarded with prized bragging rights. I have yet to experience the event, but friends have described it as both insanely chaotic and exhilarating. People crowd into every available inch of space, standing shoulder to shoulder, sometimes on shoulders, waiting for hours to catch a glimpse of the action that lasts barely a minute.

Crowds watching the Palio in Piazza del Campo.

The rise of the Venetian Republic saw the creation of another of Italy's awe-inspiring public squares, Piazza San Marco (St. Mark's Square), right in the heart of Venice. Napoleon has been credited with calling it 'the most elegant drawing-room in Europe'. Its offerings are many. Colonnade-fronted stores and elegant cafes decorate the square's borders while the Campanile (bell tower) draws eyes upward. The ornate Byzantine architecture of Basilica di San Marco (St. Mark's Basilica) provides a breathtaking punctuation mark for the Piazza, if any is required. There could be few places more delightful to enjoy a coffee or aperitivo, especially with live music from surrounding cafes adding to the ambience. Of note is historic Caffè Florian, considered the oldest coffee house in continuous operation in Italy, where literary greats such as Lord Byron, Goethe, and Dickens were frequent visitors.

Despite its challenges, I loved Venice. The first time I was there happened to be just after a massive storm had swept through the region, helping to freshen the air and flush the canals. My sister and I walked everywhere, happily getting lost many times over, although with signature landmarks at every turn, you could never get terribly lost.

The bell tower in Piazza San Marco.

We also took the vaporetto everywhere—the reasonably priced, albeit often packed, public mode of transportation, akin to city buses elsewhere. Do not mistake these for the more expensive water taxis or the gondolas complete with singing gondoliers. You can quickly distinguish them based on price.

The Renaissance ushered in a new wave of building. Upon being ordained in 1458, Pope Pius II commissioned a rebuilding of his native Tuscan village of Corsignano, renamed Pienza (City of Pius), as an ideal Renaissance city. He was among the first to apply modern urban planning concepts, honouring the era's ideals of rationalism and humanism, and adhering to a long-term development plan rather than the somewhat ad hoc planning practices of the Middle Ages. A decidedly Renaissance style was also adopted, using geometric grid patterns, and featuring symmetry and clean, simple lines.

The sculptor and architect Bernardo Rossellino was commissioned to design the central piazza, Piazza Pio II, considered by many to be one of the finest examples of a grand Renaissance piazza. The architect treated the town square as if it were a grand living room, its walls the facades of Pienza's main structures, such as the Cathedral, and Palazzo Piccolomini, the Pope's summer residence. The surrounding buildings provide both a visual and physical sense of enclosure that reinforces a welcome sense of inclusion for those wandering through.

We have enjoyed sharing this little piece of Tuscany with several friends, sampling wine along the way. An equal part of the fascination is Pienza's location in the heart of Val d'Orcia. Both the town and valley are UNESCO World Heritage sites. Recognised today as the home of Renaissance urban planning, the design principles used in the building of Pienza in the fifteenth century have been modelled in towns and cities throughout Europe and North America. The valley is admired for its quintessential Tuscan vistas, with rolling hills lined with vineyards and olive groves and punctuated by rows of cypress trees.

Although far from the scale and historical significance of the other piazzas I have mentioned, the tiny hamlet of Bagno Vignoni, also in Val d'Orcia, is worth a note. Its distinctive central piazza consists of a series of ancient stone buildings, some with colonnades, surrounding a central Renaissance-era thermal pool. Although the pool is not open to the public, it is possible to make your way down a nearby hill and bathe for free in a thermal pool below town. It took my girlfriends and me some exploring to find this tranquil spot, but it was well worth the hike.

In addition to soaking our tourist-weary feet in the warm mineral water, we had the 'bonus' of being entertained by a local. After apparently smoking some 'erbe', he was happy to prance around nude while singing an unfamiliar Italian song. After this amusing experience, we enjoyed an evening meal back in town, at a restaurant fringing the water-filled piazza. We were interested in trying some of the local fare and were not disappointed. One dish that stood out was a Tuscan classic, *pappardelle con ragu di cinghiale* (broad, flat pasta noodles with wild boar meat sauce).

Capitoline Hill is the smallest of the seven hills of Rome yet is of considerable religious and political importance. It is home to Piazza del Campidoglio. Michelangelo was commissioned to revive this square, which had been in decline since the fall of the Roman Empire, and to create a true civic plaza that would revitalise Rome and symbolise its grandeur. Despite its state of disrepair and asymmetrical shape, Michelangelo used his artistic genius to design a piazza that is elegant and aesthetically pleasing, turning its back on the ancient ruins of the Roman Forum and opening up to the modern city instead. The present-day Piazza is surrounded by palatial buildings that define the now harmonious space on three sides, creating a virtual outdoor room, open to the sky above and to the city below via a sweeping staircase, but also enclosed and protected.

Perhaps the grandest, and certainly one of the world's most famous town squares, is Piazza San Pietro (St. Peter's Square) in Vatican City. The Piazza is enveloped on either side by Bernini's semi-circular colonnades that appear to offer a universal embrace to visitors. I've visited on numerous occasions and even as a non-Catholic stand in awe every time. The Piazza does seem to want to wrap its arms around you, while at the same time allowing you to stand back and absorb the beauty and grandeur of the Basilica.

Bernini's colonnades enveloping
St. Peter's Square.

Many piazzas are known for occasions when crowds assemble, be it a celebration or a memorial, a concert or a horse race. At other times they are simply a convenient place to meet or hold the weekly market. Even small villages have a central piazza or smaller piazzetta—a place where locals will congregate, where everyone from young to old will linger (often with gelato in hand), where they will meet for their morning coffee and evening aperitivo. *As New York Times* columnist Michael Kimmelman put it, the essential function of public squares is 'sociability'; when well-designed, people gravitate to them to socialise in various ways, planned and unplanned, formal and informal.

Just as it is at the heart of daily life for Italians, the piazza is symbolic of why I was drawn to Italy. Its role in cultivating community, where people go to socialise and to feel a sense of connection and belonging, goes to the core of why I fell in love with Italy. And although I had visited and admired all the spectacular piazzas noted above, and many more, it was not until I did more reading that I fully grasped the impact town squares can have on their visitors, and how their design facilitates the socialisation that Italians seem born to embrace, and that I was so attracted to.

Creating a Sense of Community

While reading about the history of the Italian piazza, I came across a fascinating perspective on the role of the piazza in Italian society. It was in an essay by Ghigo DiTommaso, an architect and urban designer transplanted from his hometown of Bologna to San Francisco. The author saw the piazza as the heart of Italy's 'thriving public life' and set out to better understand how it worked to serve this purpose.

DiTommaso laments that a fascination with Italy's architecture, rather than a focus on the people-centred principles behind the design of its public spaces, has too often resulted in poor implementation of the concept in the United States. Squares and plazas may have started to look more like their

Italian counterparts but had none of the substance; they did not serve as centres of public life as in Italy, or as their architects had envisioned.

Using the vibrant Piazza Maggiore in Bologna as his inspiration and comparing it to San Jose's City Hall Plaza complex that 'aspired to serve as the new Agora for Silicon Valley', the author unpacks what he recognised as key elements of successful public space design. DiTommaso describes his hometown piazza as follows:

> It is the heart of the city's daily life; a place of constant teeming yet composed activity that sleeps only when the city sleeps. The piazza is the primary destination for all people, regardless of their social strata or race in a now more multicultural Italian society. It is always the place to go, whether on an ordinary day or on those special occasions in which we congregate to celebrate, or to protest. Having served this role throughout the city's history, the piazza is also the soul of its collective memory and the most potent symbol of the city itself.

By contrast, a decade after opening, San Jose's City Hall Plaza feels 'barren', he said.

In his effort to understand why these seemingly similar spaces were performing so differently, DiTommaso concludes that the City Hall Plaza 'overlooks a series of spatial principles that are rarely missing in any of the thousands of Italian piazzas in which you might find yourself enjoying a gelato'. He identifies three key principles.

The first of these is location. To create a thriving centre for a city's public life, the piazza should be positioned in the heart of the city, the space around which a city is organised. Second, a piazza should serve the public and its urban paths, not the other way around. It should be a 'node for pre-existing pedestrian patterns', not a barrier to movement; a porous place through which people pass and interact, not simply retreat to. Most intriguingly, he suggests, the Italian piazza offers a sense of possibility—'the opportunity to change your path and perhaps your mind on what you want to do', leading to unexpected interactions with people doing entirely different things from you. In complete contrast to Piazza Maggiore, DiTommaso notes that the City Hall Plaza is located on the outskirts of San Jose's city centre and is disconnected from the main urban paths that define its downtown core. The result is a space that is almost devoid of life beyond City Hall operating hours.

His third key principle is, as he puts it, 'active and permeable ground floors'. While central piazzas are typically enclosed by a city's most important civic and religious buildings, the piazza must also include buildings and activities at a 'human scale'; a mixture of shops, cafes, bars, restaurants, and even houses that 'encourage human encounters' and add life to an otherwise static space. The 'ground-floor life-suckers' as he calls the multi-level parking garage, big-box retailers, and gas stations around the City Hall Plaza just did not fit the bill for DiTommaso.

As DiTommaso sees it, when these key structural elements are incorporated into its design, the piazza effectively becomes the stage upon which 'the spectacle of public life is set to unfold'. As he and others have noted, a successful urban piazza effectively becomes the town's theatre, with those who flock there choosing to take the role of the actor on some occasions, and the spectator on others.

I was fascinated to learn that a piazza's design could have such an influence on our use of public space, as well as on how we feel in the process. I could also see how they were drawing me in. With nothing to do, I would wander down to the piazza to absorb the atmosphere and enjoy the community that surrounded me, like a theatre in the round. And with friends to meet, we would arrange to connect in the piazza. My life in Italy began to revolve around the piazza, and revisiting my piazza experiences throughout Italy, the pieces of the puzzle were fitting together. My research was mirroring my emotions back to me. What I was feeling is exactly what the designers of these public spaces wanted me to feel. How Italian life plays out in the piazza, and more importantly, how these durable elements of Italy's urban scape help create and sustain the social fabric of the community, is entirely by design.

Favourite Piazza Experiences

After visiting many such square across Italy, several stand out. I found it easier to get a true sense of a place that is not overflowing with tours and tourists (even though I was one of them). While Piazza Navona may be overflowing with people in August and seem full of life, it is unlikely that many would be Romans. Most locals will surely have escaped the sweltering heat for the mountains, or the sea, or even just a small house in the country. You won't find sane Romans in Rome in August if it can be helped.

I'm most familiar with the piazza area in the heart of Fondi, having spent more time here than elsewhere in Italy. Spending extended periods in one place also allows its true nature to unfold at its own pace. The people in the piazza and surrounding cafes were locals, living their lives as Italians across the country do, and I had a front row seat for the show.

With the help of our friends who introduced me to Fondi, this was a place where everything a main piazza is intended to be seemed to present itself. I socialized with old friends and met new ones, watched others interact as they ran into friends and neighbours, enjoyed listening to music floating in from the nearby amphitheatre as I sipped on my Aperol Spritz, and generally just soaked up the atmosphere and events that played out around me. And although I didn't know it at the time, the design and functioning of this public space were helping me feel like I was all the while at home with friends and family.

In Fondi's main piazza, with the Castello behind me.

Another authentic piazza experience I recall was in the village of Cella Monte, in the Monferrato wine area of Piedmont. I discovered a small piazza at the top of town, including a cafe and restaurant with an inviting patio and extended views across the valley. I passed by it almost every day for three weeks, either on foot or bicycle. While working at La Casaccia, a nearby agriturismo, I found the cafe a comforting spot to visit at the end of a long day or on a rare afternoon off.

Once, on my way back from a lengthy bike ride through the surrounding hills, on impulse I stopped for a late lunch. Although it was after 2:00 p.m. and they were technically closed, the owners willingly made me one of my favourite lunches, *insalata mista e verdure grigliate* (mixed salad and grilled vegetables). Capped off with a glass of local Barbera del Monferrato, I could not have felt more content.

On other occasions I visited for an aperitivo or coffee, and it was just as I had experienced in villages across Italy—different people came and went, but always the old men were there. Even on days the cafe was closed, men would meet outside and play cards, or sit in a big circle and socialise. I enjoyed assuming my place as a spectator at one of the picnic tables. Following their routines made me feel a small part of this daily heartbeat of the community.

During a visit to Venice with my mother and sister, we found an ideal abode close to Piazza San Marco but away from the crowds. I fell in love with the area around our apartment. It felt like we had our own little *vicino* (neighbourhood) in the city's heart, complete with its own piazzetta, cafe, post office, pizzeria, and fruit market. I have always loved that about bigger cities: the ability to feel tucked away, but in the middle of things at the same time. While the sense of community was refreshing, what made the experience even more memorable was when the barista at our local cafe said *Dimmi!* when I walked in one morning, meaning 'Tell me what I can get you'. This is a more casual way of greeting a customer (the colloquial version of *mi dica*), usually reserved for regulars or friends. Wow! I'm a local! Not really, but that is how it made me feel. And I liked it!

One piazza experience I recall with fondness took place in the tiny hilltop hamlet of Campodimele. Situated in the Aurunci Mountains of Lazio, about halfway between Rome and Naples, the hamlet is barely more than a small cluster of medieval houses, many built right into the protective stone wall that encircles the village. The piazza is also small and appears to drop off the edge of the cliff, offering a perfect place to enjoy views of the serene Liri Valley below. This visit turned out to be market day. There was only a handful of vendors on hand, but as the four of us sat in a nearby cafe it looked like everyone in the village came by at one point or another. I recall an elderly lady. She took what seemed like ten minutes to get up a slight slope in the road beside where we were seated, had a rest when she got to the top, and then began her shopping.

On another visit we wandered through the cobblestone streets that meander out from the little square and I swear everyone we met wanted us to talk, and at length. They were all older women, two of them even inviting us in for coffee. Joe understood their dialect and was able to converse with them, but we declined the coffee. Looking back, I wish we'd taken them up on their offers. What interesting stories we might have heard.

Filomena and Gord along a back alley in Campodimele.

The Effect

It was difficult to absorb all the technical talk I was reading, about something as 'simple' as a town square. But having stood in the centre of so many piazzas, experiencing the draw and feeling the emotions their designers were hoping to elicit, I came to understand why they hold such an attraction for Italians as a destination for the 'spectacle of public life'. Even as a *straniera* (foreigner), I cannot now conceive of Italian towns without their central piazza. As I have learned from my travels, socialisation is at the heart of Italian culture, and the more time one spends in Italy, the more obvious it becomes how public spaces such as the piazza play an integral role in this cultural imperative.

To watch this 'sociability' play out across Italy was a learning process, and my research on the history of public squares backs up my own impressions. Just as was intended by city planners centuries ago, the function of the piazza as a 'community destination' has allowed me to connect with locals, feel included, and learn about the everyday lives of real Italians. And they are great for enjoying a Spritz and people-watching too.

While Canada's weather is not as accommodating as Italy's, it has become more common for Canadian neighbourhoods to create thoughtful gathering places through purposeful design. We have festivals and events in our main downtown squares, and streets turned into pedestrian-only zones for weekend or evening markets that attract throngs of people and constitute social outings for many. Canadian cities are changing in this regard, and I expect the same can be said for cities across North America. Hopefully before long, what an Italian friend told me about her hometown of Trieste will not be so far from the truth here: 'You don't even need to make plans. You just go down to the piazza, and you will meet friends and will always have fun!'

CHAPTER 8

Il Mercato – The Market

Through its markets you will discover the true sole of a city.

—Anonymous

The piazza and the mercato are like two sides of a sheet of music—you will find the rhythm of the city in both. Having been around for as long as humans have engaged in trade, the local market was often a catalyst for later development of the Italian piazza as we know it today. The concentration of retailers in one place had many advantages. Vendors could keep an eye on their competition, customers had choice, and municipal governments could regulate them as they saw fit.

The history and culture of a city is reflected in the local products and explosion of scents you will experience at the market. Depending on the size and type of market, you will find pretty much everything you need, and more: fresh produce and local cheeses, trendy clothes and handbags, even shoes adorned with sparkly embellishments. And despite the convenience of supermarkets, Italians still love to shop at their local market—it is an integral part of the Italian way of life. We can learn about Italy's past from its museums and monuments, but head to the market to learn about the everyday life of Italians today.

As important as the consistent quality and variety of products that markets offer, is the opportunity for neighbours to meet and visit on a social level. More than just a place to shop, it is a destination—an arena where friends, family, and community come together. The mercato attracts people from all walks of life. There is no barrier of wealth or class; everyone is looking for the freshest tomatoes and the best prices. In crowded markets, young children stay close to their mothers as they scan the fruit and vegetables or hold a dress up to check its size. The men, on the other hand, seem to prefer to find the items they came for and then sit on a bench in the shade to watch and wait.

While you can find daily markets in larger cities, smaller centres generally have a designated market day (often going back years) and frequenting them became a mini passion of mine. I would go out of my way to coordinate my visit to a town with its market day. The mercato added an extra level of appeal—an opportunity to see the community in action. It seemed like a social event, a form of recreation, and being in the middle of a market made me feel like I was taking part in the daily life of a town rather than just observing from the sidelines.

A memorable market experience took place in the picturesque Sicilian town of Taormina. Among other things, this tourist-friendly town is known for its Teatro Antico, an ancient Greco-Roman amphitheatre that continues to be used for performances and other events. My only disappointment when visiting was that we weren't able to get our hands on tickets to the Il Volo (an Italian operatic pop trio) performance taking place in the theatre that night. Not surprisingly, it was completely sold out. The amphitheatre sits on a terrace overlooking the Ionian Sea and provides dramatic views along Sicily's east coast, and even across to mainland Italy on clear days. It also would have been an incredible spot to enjoy the sunset. *La prossima volta!* Next time.

After a morning hike to the village of Castelmola, a little gem in the hills above Taormina, we discovered a covered market happening just down the street from our apartment. We were in search of items for lunch. I asked one vendor about her olives, and out came samples. It was the same for her deli meats and cheeses. She even gave us some bread to eat with it, and a little plastic cup of vino to wash it down. Her husband outdid himself by making us espresso to cap it all off. By the time we were done I wasn't sure I even needed lunch!

Unlike Campo de' Fiori, which has hosted a market since the 1800s, and nearby Piazza Navona, both tourist favourites in Rome, my Roman friend explained that the Testaccio Mercato is where many locals shop. The area (located southwest of the Colosseum) sits on an artificial mound, composed largely of broken clay vessels dating back to the Roman Empire. A local institution for over eighty years, the market's mix of fresh food stalls and fishmongers, as well as non-food items and plentiful street food, draws people from all parts of Rome. As my friend showed us around, vendors she knew would offer a friendly greeting. On occasion she would embrace friends she ran into with the customary *bacio* on each cheek. Samples were offered when we stopped for a closer look, and the vendors were continually adjusting their produce to ensure it looked as good as it tasted.

A suggestion though—don't touch the produce. It is frowned upon and simply not done. Rather, talk to the vendor. If you want peaches that are ready to eat today, let them know. If there is a piece of meat or fish you like the look of, point. And if you don't know what an item is, or what you would do with it, ask. I loved getting involved in these types of conversations—another great way to practice *il mio italiano*.

The street markets in Palermo, the capital of Sicily and a busy port town, played to all the senses like nothing I'd experienced before. This ancient city is a cultural melting pot and an open history book, displaying the layers of civilisation that conquerors brought to the island, starting with the Phoenicians as far back as the eleventh century BC. Owing to its history, Sicily was ethnically diverse from the outset. Christians, Jews, Muslims, Arabs, Byzantine Greeks, and native Sicilians have all called the island home. Not surprisingly, their markets offer equally diverse foods, with flavours and aromas to match.

The Ballarò food market, for example, is like an ancient Arab-style souk. It's a hectic place where you'll hear a constant barrage of vendors trying to out-yell each other and where you can sample inexpensive Sicilian street food such as its famous *arancini* (fried stuffed rice balls), baked onions, and *panelle* (fritters made with chickpea flour).

Here, and across the central area we visited, we saw vendors diligently stoking their fires during the afternoon, to ensure scorching heat for dinner customers. In the evening they would barbeque various meats, often on sticks like kebabs, or sausages served on buns. Their barbeques lit up the streets, attracting crowds waiting their turn. We came across several such vendors as we wandered back from dinner. There were also several in a piazza near our apartment. I was intrigued by what I saw, yet hesitant at the same time. I must confess that I didn't sample anything. Whether out of fear or uncertainty, it was an opportunity lost.

Palermo man barbecuing street food.

I'm reminded of a story about a friend who has a passion for Italian cuisine. When Nancy was in Sicily, she would go every morning to the local market in the tiny village where she was staying. On one visit, a vendor displaying fresh octopus succeeded in attracting her attention. She shrugged, explaining that she would have no idea what to do with it. The next thing Nancy knew, she was getting a lesson on cleaning octopus. The vendor made her clean several until he was satisfied her fish would pass inspection. I'm not sure she came home with any recipes, but I could tell from her story that she had loved every minute.

Speaking of lively fish vendors, it's a toss-up for me between a fish market in Naples and one in the Sicilian city of Catania. Both were exciting to visit, albeit quite 'aromatic' shall we say, and certainly noisy. There seemed to be every type of fish on display, as well as buckets of seafood such as *cozze* (mussels) and *polpo* (octopus). I was intrigued by the displays, the sheer quantity of fish that was caught and sold every day, and the theatrical vendors shouting—or even singing—about their catch of the day.

Naples was the capital of the Mezzogiorno from the Middle Ages; now it is the regional capital of Campania. The historic centre of Naples, one of the largest and oldest in Europe, was designated a World Heritage site in 1997. Densely populated, it is also a city of contrasts, located on the scenic Bay of Naples with Mount Vesuvius as its backdrop while internally there is grit and graffiti, chaos and urban sprawl. I was drawn to the unconventional beauty and found inspiration wandering the labyrinth of streets, wondering what I'd find around the next corner.

Near the port, we happened upon the Porta Nolana Mercato and its famous fish market that dates from the fifteenth century. This was my first experience with singing fishmongers, and we all got a kick out of it. That said, they were serious about their business and did not have much time for curious tourists.

La Pescheria in Catania is another of Italy's famous fish markets. Located in a sunken piazza just a few blocks from the port where the fishing boats come in, and stuffed to the gills with fish, the market smells like the sea itself.

La Pesceria in Catania.

Fishmongers are here almost every morning, as were their ancestors before them, doing their best to attract buyers with their animated behaviour and loud voices. If you can deal with the apparent chaos, you will find almost every type of fish and seafood imaginable. As always, Gord found a way to use his limited Italian skills to strike up a conversation with one of the vendors selling swordfish. When I asked for a photograph, Gord's new friend handed him an enormous cleaver—to make the picture more *eccitante* (exciting), he said.

I should also mention the Rialto Fish Market in Venice, where fishmongers have been hawking their fish to Venetians for centuries. Starting at dawn, you can buy cuttlefish and other local favourites just off the boats. It is closed Sundays and Mondays, which is apparently why Venetians don't order fish at restaurants on Mondays. Buyer beware!

While markets generally energize me and add interest to any shopping experience, I can't help thinking about the life of some of the vendors. This is obviously not exclusive to Italian markets, but it hit home one time when I was visiting a massage therapist in Fondi. She had recently married, but rarely saw her husband. His family ran a fruit stand in Rome that was open every day except Sunday, and Monday morning. Referred to as a *corriere* (courier), he awoke each morning at 4:00 a.m. and, with his produce in tow, made the 90-minute trek into Rome to begin his workday. By the time her husband returned home in the evening, he was lucky to get four hours of sleep before it started all over again. I was humbled hearing their story.

CHAPTER 9

Rituals and Traditions

Ritual affirms the common patterns, the values, the shared joys, risks, sorrows, and changes that bind a community together. Ritual links together our ancestors and descendants, those who went before with those who will come after us.

—Starhawk

Social practices, rituals, and festive events are intentional activities that structure and shape our lives. They are inclusive occasions practised around the world, albeit in forms as diverse as the human experience. They may vary from small gatherings to large celebrations—even a handshake can be considered a ritual. Our ancestors used ritual to create bonds of kinship that were essential for survival. And while we no longer need them to serve this purpose, rituals are still an essential part of our lives. They tie us to our heritage, building bridges between the past and future, helping us understand where we came from and where we're going. Through ritual we build family and community, celebrate important events, mark the passing of seasons, and express joy and sorrow. Rituals offer a needed sense of stability and continuity and remind us of the interconnectedness of life.

As rituals are handed down through generations, they become traditions, a word derived from the Latin *tradere*, meaning to transmit, hand over, give for safekeeping. Both are a means through which a community expresses adherence to shared values and a communal identity, reminding us who we are and what we value.

Life in Italy is teeming with ritual. And, while not exclusive to Italy by any stretch, it was my experiences in Italy that helped me better understand the value of time-honoured traditions that bind us together. I recognised how they help us connect with family, with our community, even with ourselves, and how they remind us that there is something beyond our own story.

Below are some of the enduring rituals and traditions that I experienced during my travels. Some were planned, others unexpected pleasures I stumbled across. Big or small, they made me feel connected to where I was in a more robust, richer sense. They helped cultivate meaningful relationships and bonds that nourished my *anima* (soul).

La Passeggiata – Evening Stroll

It is difficult to talk about life in the piazza without also describing its close cousin, the *passeggiata*. You will rarely find one without the other. The word comes from the verb *passeggiare*, to go for a slow walk or stroll. When Italians ask if you want to *fare una passeggiata*, they are asking you to join them for something akin to a promenade, usually centred around pedestrian friendly routes leading to the main piazza. But they encapsulate so much more.

Whether you are in a big city or small village, you will find this tradition practised religiously throughout Italy. It gets going around 5:00 p.m., as shops and cafes raise their shutters and swing open their doors. You will encounter it on weekend evenings, but often on weekdays as well, following work and before dinner. Entire families, couples, friends, stream into the streets, usually with close attention being paid to their appearance despite it being a casual occasion—and always with stylish footwear, even if just trendy runners. That said, as with the markets, the passeggiata does not discriminate based on class. The weekend passeggiata is often the social event of the week for many, and it does not cost a thing to participate.

Some say the movement and fresh air simply aid digestion after long Sunday lunches, or help work up an appetite for dinner. But it is also an opportunity to socialise, to catch up with the latest news (or gossip), to see and be seen. From a cultural perspective, informal social events like the passeggiata are viewed as a means of involving everyone in the life of the community, reinforcing a sense of belonging. People of all ages participate in one way or another; babies in their strollers, young children walking hand in hand with a parent, couples or friends linked arm in arm. Young girls with attitude will strut their stuff down the middle of the pedestrian zone, which is often the main passeggiata route. The elderly may sit at cafes, or on benches in the piazza, and wait to be spoken to as they quietly look on. Amongst those in attendance, some are the spectators, others the entertainment.

My first recollection of a passeggiata was in Naples, with my husband and brother, during one of my earliest visits to Italy. We'd spent most of our day exploring the city, being the tourists that we were. We visited the sights, ate pizza margherita in the streets, managed to get kicked off the balcony of Palazzo Reale (a story for another time), stopped for an expensive aperitivo down by the marina, and generally squeezed as much out of the day as we could. As we distanced ourselves from the bar-filled marina area we came upon the eye-catching Galleria Umberto I. Built in the Art Nouveau style of the late nineteenth century, it was a centrepiece for the revitalisation of Naples. The covered shopping arcade was modelled on the fashionable Galleria

Vittorio Emanuele II in Milan, including a mix of shops, cafes and open space on the ground floor level, and apartments above. It also served as a passageway between different parts of the city, connecting the San Carlo Theatre on one side with Via Toledo on the other.

Metal and glass ceiling of Galleria Umberto I.

After admiring the structure, with its vaulted ceilings made of glass and steel and a huge central dome, we drifted onto Via Toledo, a major shopping street by day and a popular pedestrian zone by night. We were wide-eyed tourists and at this point I had never heard of a passeggiata. I found out about the nuances of this ritual after the fact, recognising that I had been woefully underdressed, and I don't even want to think about the shoes

I was wearing. But none of that mattered. It felt like we were part of a spectacle of sorts on a busy outdoor runway. We were surrounded by crowds of people, fashionably dressed in anything from jeans to smart suits and dresses. Everyone was strolling along the broad sidewalk and down the middle of the street. It was a somewhat chaotic arrangement, but it all worked. The actors in this play seemed to be enjoying everything, whether window shopping or eating gelato, and themselves of course. Perhaps it was just a snapshot in time and place, but this introduction to a traditional aspect of Italian life pulled me in.

Many years and many passeggiata later I was pleasantly surprised by a similar though smaller-scale experience in Campobasso (Molise), where my first Italian teacher's family was from. We only had a day to spare, so we spent most of it poking around town, finishing up at the castle. It was dark when we eventually made our way down, and to my delight the street behind our B&B was awash with people. In a blog post, I wrote how the streets were full for several blocks, and how it was fun to watch—the younger generation congregating with friends, elders crisply dressed, everyone socialising. I noted that it was often groups of men and women gathering separately. (The secret of a successful marriage perhaps?)

That post sums up my passeggiata experiences, irrespective of region—everyday occasions made special, everyone out socialising and having a good time in whatever manner suits them. I know appearances can be deceiving, but even for those who are feeling lonely, I can't think of a better opportunity to turn that around than by heading to the piazza. It's a way to feel more involved with the world around you, and hopefully it will help put a smile on your face. My preference was to walk along the side rather than up the middle, more comfortable as a spectator than the centre of attention, but there is a spot for everyone.

Evening passeggiata in Campobasso.

It's Aperitivo Time Somewhere

Notwithstanding the intensely regional character that epitomises much of Italian culture, there are observances you will find practised throughout the country. Along with Sunday mass and calcio, aperitivo is one such ritual. Like passeggiata, it's another opportunity to meet and socialise, build friendships, stay involved. The term derives from the Latin word for 'opener', and while the hour for 'aperitivo time' can vary depending where you are, no one will argue that it is a pre-meal drink. The original idea was to gather in early evening to enjoy good company and conversation while sipping a cocktail and munching on a few small bites. Traditionally intended to whet one's appetite for dinner rather than replace it, the ritual seems to have evolved to serve both purposes. And while the tradition may be common throughout Italy, there are certainly regional variations.

Perhaps because the tradition originated in northern Italy, one tends to find more substantial food offerings north of Rome, as was the case in the trendy Navigli district of Milan.

While I'm sure there are questionable establishments catering to tourists who descend on the area, we managed to find a tucked-away place that served our drinks with a fresh sampling of finger food. We paid more for our drinks, as expected, but found the offerings worth the price. Unfortunately, I managed to spill my Spritz while trying to take a photograph, but my mood improved considerably when our waitress, who had watched my mini fiasco, was quick to bring a refill.

The Navigli district of Milan.

Cicchetti is a local term for small savoury bar snacks or side dishes served in Venice, typically eaten with fingers and toothpicks while lingering around the bar. The range of offerings can include items such as fried rice balls filled with cheese and tiny sandwiches, or even small samplings of full-course plates. It was tricky to figure out the process, but by watching other patrons I learned that once you paid for a drink you were welcomed to take a small plate of items to nibble on.

In Ostia, the former port of ancient Rome and home of its fascinating archaeological site, Ostia Antica, we paid a higher price for our drinks but were treated to a sizeable platter of finger food. I remember appreciating the variety of items I got to try (not to mention the side show from a young boy who amused himself by shimmying up a nearby lamp pole while waiting for his parents).

I experienced a similar practice in Turin (Piedmont), the first capital city of Italy, and for centuries before that the heart of the Duchy of Savoy. Originally settled by the Taurini, a Celtic people, and later by the Romans, Turin is rich in history and culture. With the Po River running through it and the Alps as its backdrop, it is also striking. A mix of Baroque and Art Nouveau architecture combined with broad, well-lit streets, sets the historic centre of Turin apart. In the more traditional medieval towns further south (such as Siena, San Gimignano, and Monteriggioni in Tuscany), streets tend to be narrow and haphazard and the Romanesque architecture heavy and stocky. For 10 euro (several years ago now) I was offered a drink and a visit to a buffet that even included pasta. Thinking back, I may have gone up for a second helping, which I hope was considered acceptable. I certainly wouldn't want to ruin my *bella figura* (or leave a bad impression as Italians would say)!

I'm also remembering an amusing situation on the island of Sicily. I have not introduced you to Maria and her sister-in-law yet, but it still makes me laugh thinking about an afternoon I spent with them in their hometown of Delia. We went out to see if Maria could get me a much-needed appointment with her hairdresser. He could see me in about an hour, so we decided to head to *il bar* (as Italians call cafes) for a drink. Maria laughed that it is always men—*sempre gli uomini*—parked at the tables, but it didn't dissuade her from sitting down amidst them. I liked her style!

In Fondi, in central Italy, you are unlikely to get more than chips and peanuts, perhaps with an occasional olive in your drink. We did find a few exceptions for those willing to pay a little more, and the marginally higher price was certainly worth it for the variety of finger food served. In Fondi's defence, I would add that drinks seemed to be stronger than the watered-down ones I've come to expect in some larger tourist centres. I'm not much of a drinker but can usually manage to get through an Aperol Spritz without difficulty (Aperol, prosecco, and a splash of mineral water). But in Fondi I usually felt *un po' ubriaca* (tipsy) after just one drink.

Lenola is a cute town in the hills above Fondi. I love the quaintness of its historic centre, the sweeping stone stairway leading from Santa Maria del Colle Basilica at the top of town down to its central piazza, and the village's tranquil feel. Joe tells me that when he was young his family would head up to Lenola for their summer holiday, to beat the humidity and heat in the valley below. His dad would bike downhill into town every morning, to save money on bus fare, and after work take his bike on the bus back to Lenola. I've biked both ways and would not want to be making the uphill ride home every day after work, especially on a one-speed bicycle that Luigi would have been using back in the 1950s.

We drove there looking for pizza one evening but ended up instead with an enticing aperitivo platter (fresh ricotta, sausage, hard local cheese, beans, veggies, bread, olives) for just 10 euro. Along with our drinks, we had an engaging conversation with the woman serving us, who was literally moving back to Germany the next day. She found Lenola too small for her liking—everyone knew everyone's business, she said. Welcome to Italy.

Perhaps my most memorable aperitivo was on Elba Island. We were sailing with friends and moored in Porto Azzurro for our last night on the island. I'd met Salvatore in Turin at the World Masters Games, a huge sporting event for age groups ranging from 30 and up. Many participants had been elite athletes in their heyday, my sister included, but to qualify for these games you just needed to be of a certain vintage.

Sal was a childhood friend of our coach, Joe D. With his warm smile and pleasant demeanour, I knew instantly that I liked him. We stayed in touch via social media and, five years later, when I said we'd be sailing around Elba, he extended a warm welcome to visit him. I knew the offer was sincere, but I was hesitant. Unlike my super sociable husband and brother, I tend to be on the reserved side—finding excuses not to follow up on such offers. I would tell myself that they are too busy, or that it would be awkward because I don't really know them. Thankfully, I did not let that internal dialogue get the better of me this time. In Italy I wanted to experience it all, and the only way to do that was to seek out authentic experiences centred around locals rather than tourists, and traditions rather than trends.

I arranged with Sal to meet us at the marina, and after hugs and introductions the four of us piled into his vehicle. Our destination was the state penitentiary. This rather unorthodox location, where Sal was director of accounting, only added to the intrigue. Following a tour of the area authorised for visitors, we went up to Sal's home on the grounds. Here we put together a simple plate of nibbles, climbed up to the rooftop terrace, opened a bottle of wine, and enjoyed our aperitivo with a panoramic view of the harbour.

I remember Sal's comment as we looked out over the water. Spreading his arms from east to west, he remarked on the view. From here, he said, *Posso vedere l'alba al mattino e il tramonto la sera. Non posso chiedere di più* (I can see the sunrise in the morning and sunset in the evening. I can't ask for more). It was heart-warming to meet someone so content with life. Shortly after we returned home, I received a picture of Sal grilling up a variety of meats on his barbeque for friends. He said that is what we would be treated to next time we visit. Count me in! And, for sure, we will be staying to see his beloved sunset.

With Sal in Porto Azzurro.

The quality or quantity of food offered during aperitivo is not the point here. Nor is the stiffness of the drink. What I loved about all these experiences was the opportunity to participate in a ritual that gets people out in the streets, greeting old friends and making new ones, and interacting over conversation, food, and drink. Rather than just doing my own thing, I was doing what locals were doing, taking part in their rituals.

Le Sagre – Celebrations and Festivals

Sagre (plural of *sagra*), are another integral part of Italian culture. The word derives from the Latin *sacra*, meaning holy, which illustrates their original purpose. Many such festivals are dedicated to saints. And while most saints' days may go unnoticed in less traditionally Catholic countries, in many towns and villages across Italy the feast of their local patron saint is the major event of the year. Such events often combine solemn processions through the streets with festivities such as races, open-air dances, special meals and markets, and extravagant fireworks.

I can think of several occasions where we were held up in traffic because of religious processions, and one occasion that really should be left to memory, where the reverse happened. We were dropping my brother off at Termini, the central train station in Rome, and somehow managed to get in the middle of a religious procession. The decidedly significant factor in this case was that the procession included *il Papa* (the Pope). The carabinieri were not amused.

Other sagre grew out of local country fairs or ancient pagan rituals. Many celebrate food. Taste buds may be lured by delicacies such as chestnuts and white truffles in the North, or the aroma of lemons and olives in the South. And you are equally likely to find sagre involving every variety of produce in between. As with their religious sagre, towns and cities go all out. Streets are decorated, processions organised, and there will undoubtedly be singing and dancing. While most include vendors selling their goods, you may also find tastings of local produce or cooking demonstrations, even art or dance lessons.

Some sagre have grown into major international events, such as Venice's *Carnevale*, the International White Truffle Fair in Alba (Piedmont), and *Festival delle Sagre* (Festival of Festivals) in nearby Asti, but many more remain local affairs. I was close to both Alba and Asti while working at La Casaccia and was hoping to attend at least one of their festivals, but unfortunately the timing conflicted with obligations at the agriturismo. You will hear more about La Casaccia, and the special family that owns it. And I will make plans to visit Alba and Asti another time.

There have been a few festas that really stood out for me. The first was in Marta, a medieval village in northern Lazio that sits along the shores of Lake Bolsena. I was fortunate to be staying at a nearby B&B and joined my host and her friends for the *Festa della Madonna del Monte* (Feast of the Madonna of the Mountain), also known as the *Festa delle Passate* (Feast of the Past). This ancient religious festival takes place every May and I gladly accepted the invitation despite having no idea what it would entail. As we approached the small town, it seemed to be inundated—there were cars everywhere. We managed to find a parking spot (of sorts) and made our way into town.

The festival is a celebration and an offering to the Madonna, mother of Jesus, in thanks for the harvest from the land and the lake. The day was unlike anything I'd experienced. Ceremonial riders dressed in simple attire (black riding breeches, boots and hats, white shirts, and bright blue sashes) led the procession atop large horses, followed by decorated wagons and floats, interspersed with men and youngsters on foot. The wagons were loaded with the bounty for which they were giving thanks: wheat and bread, fish, prosciutto, cheeses, wines, fruits, and vegetables.

Groups would parade by with their arms waving, most wearing white shirts, simple straw or black felt hats, and colourful bandanas. Periodically, they would stop and sing a verse (of what I'm not sure) before continuing. I remember the huge smiles, especially on the faces of wide-eyed children, both those in the parade and the young spectators lining the crowded streets. Residents with homes along the route cosied up on their balconies, clapping and cheering as floats paraded by, at times throwing out flower petals like confetti. We stood and watched in appreciation, then moved along with the crowd, eventually making our way up to the Chiesa della Madonna del Monte where the procession was to end. But I quickly learned there was more to come.

After the religious rituals concluded, participants began offering their produce, not just to the gods but to anyone who wanted to partake. Some were slicing pieces off huge legs of prosciutto, others from rounds of cheese. There was bread of all shapes and sizes to go along, and glasses of wine to wash it down. Whether a resident or tourist, participant or spectator, these offerings seemed to fill more than appetites and were bringing people together over something more substantial than food. The experience was many years ago, yet the memories remain fresh. I was with friends who each have a light that shines brightly, and this also shaped my response to the whole experience. I felt connected.

Young boys enjoying the Festa in Marta.

More recently, I attended the *Festa del Vino del Monferrato* (Wine Festival of Monferrato) in Casale Monferrato (Casale for short). Founded in the eighth century, Casale sits along the Po River in the hills east of Turin. It is the capital of the Monferrato wine district, one of the three main wine-producing regions of Italy. *Vendemmia* is the Italian word for wine harvest, and accordingly, the festa is also referred to as *Sagra della Vendemmia.*

After finishing work early at the agriturismo, Margherita, Antonia, and I drove to Casale for the festa. But first we went to help with a *degustazione* (wine-tasting) the city was hosting to promote local products. Producers had been asked to assist with this inaugural event, being held in the courtyard of Casale's fourteenth-century castle, but for whatever reason we were the only ones to show up. After carrying boxes and boxes of wine and wine glasses, and then washing and drying the glasses, we'd had enough and called it quits. If there were samples to be had it might have been another story but no such luck.

We did, however, take the opportunity to tour the interesting old castle, built in a hexagonal shape with four round towers and surrounded by a moat (in its glory days). From the top we had a superb view across the city. I was surprised to learn it was Margherita's first time in the castle. Sometimes as tourists we take advantage of opportunities available to us more so than when we're at home. A good lesson to remember.

After our tour we headed into the streets to explore the city ahead of the festival. We sampled *krumiri*, a type of biscotti regarded as a delicacy here, and popular throughout Italy. As the story goes, a local confectioner created these half-moon-shaped cookies to replicate the moustache of King Victor Emmanuel II and thus pay him homage. I'm not sure that visual does them justice, but we managed to devour quite a few so it obviously was not a deterrent. And, of course, gelato was a perfect accompaniment.

As Margherita made her exit to take care of errands, Antonia and I sat for aperitivo—on this occasion the good kind where we were offered an appetizing charcuterie platter to accompany our drinks. We noticed people enjoying their drinks and snacks everywhere; there were lots of options to choose from.

Then it was time for me to meet Gord. He had arrived that day on an international flight from Canada, renting a car at Malpensa Airport in Milan and driving an hour to Casale. To avoid having to find parking in the busy central area, we agreed to meet just across the river. There, we could leave the car for free and were still in easy walking distance of Piazza Castello, where the festival was taking place. I'm not sure I would have been in a partying mood after all that travel, but it ended up being an effective way for him to stay awake and make the transition to Italian time a little smoother, as well as a lot of fun.

I know Italians like their wine, but as the night rolled on the place sounded more and more like an outlandish Octoberfest! There were many varieties of wine available, including the region's signature Barbera, Grignolino, and Freisa, and various sparkling wines, all reasonably priced. And with wine you need food, of which there was plenty. Around the entire perimeter of the vast area were nothing but food stalls, all serving popular local dishes. As the evening progressed it became challenging to hear a person sitting just across the table. A ritual of singing a cheering song every time someone returned to their table with a new bottle of wine only added to the chaos, but also to the fun. I believe there were over 2,500 seats, set out in rows and rows of family-style tables under an enormous tent structure.

After a bit of schmoozing, we managed to find room at one of the long tables. I learned that the lady I sat beside was studying English, and I'm always working on my Italian, so we tested each other for amusement. I also ended up sampling some of the food they had purchased. They wanted us to try everything. The man next to us was also offering advice on the best foods to purchase. While his *fritto misto* looked tempting, it was heavy on meat, which is not my thing. I also learned that the 'meat' in this Piedmontese dish is focused on the internal organs of animals, again not my thing.

We did get a plate of *agnolotti*, a stuffed pasta typical of Piedmont, made with small pieces of flattened pasta dough folded over a meat or vegetable filling. They look a lot like ravioli to the untrained eye, but apparently there is a difference in the way they are made. Regardless, it was the perfect way to sample a local favourite.

Later we joined Margherita's friends, including a charismatic African from Mali who was working at La Casaccia. His story involved horrors you cannot imagine, but he was now safe and happily working here. The festa was a highlight of my time at La Casaccia, in part because it was such an authentic experience, and because I was able to share it with locals (and my hubby of course).

Sagra della Vendemmia, with Gord, Antonia, Margherita, and our new friends.

Speaking of too much meat, while visiting the archaeological site of ancient Norma (Lazio), which dates to 492 BC, we stumbled across a local country fair. We were too early for most of the excitement but decided to see if we could find something interesting for lunch. Although I didn't try any, I could not get over how much meat was being cooked, clearly a favourite of this farming community. Watching the men at work, it was obvious they had done this before. They were managing several types of meat on enormous grills, the resulting smoke and enticing smell drifting through the air.

One stall was offering classic Roman dishes with three types of pasta. I was familiar with *carbonara* but had never tried either of the very Roman *amatriciana* or *cacio e pepe*. I asked the ladies if I could possibly have a plate with half of each. Not only did they let me try both, but they gave me a full plate of each for the same price. Cacio e pepe (cheese and pepper) was the winner for me, although the spicier amatriciana was also good. The experience reminded me of someone I'd met at our favourite beach bar near Sperlonga. She was from Rome and was aching for Roman *amatriciana* pasta. She said it just didn't taste the same at restaurants around Sperlonga, even though we were only about a 90-minute drive from Rome.

I was sorry we couldn't stay at the fair any longer and missed a demonstration by the *butteri*. These are the traditional horsemen and cattle breeders of the Maremma, a rugged area that spans northern Lazio and southern Tuscany in addition to the Pontine Marsh area of Lazio where the fair was held. The butteri way of life, herding the long-horned Maremma cattle (one of Europe's oldest breeds) and raising their own breed of horses, dates to when the Etruscans began utilising these areas for agricultural purposes. Today these groups work to keep alive the ancient skills and culture of the legendary cowboys.

Sardinia is full of old traditions and customs, with many of its sagre based on the island's diverse cultural groups. When Gord and I were both in Sardinia, staying at Rosanna's B&B, she invited us to join her on a trip to Nuoro, in central Sardinia, for the *Sagra del Redentore* (Feast of the Redeemer). It is an interwoven celebration of religious and folk traditions, and one of Sardinia's biggest festivals. Not surprising, we arrived to find the streets congested and parking at a premium. Despite the crowds we did manage to find a good vantage point where we were able to gaze down over the lively parade making its way through the streets.

The participants wore old-style costumes, some designed for everyday life and others for ceremonies such as weddings and funerals. Rosanna noted how some groups clearly represented more affluent regions than others, pointing to gold trim, ribbons, and additional detail on some costumes. Groups would intermittently stop and entertain spectators with their traditional song and dance. It was great to have our own personal guide who was so familiar with the island's history and culture. *Grazie* Rosanna!

Staying with Rosanna on my own the following year, I attended *Bastida di Sorres*, a three-day medieval festival in a tiny hamlet called Borutta. We car-pooled with two of her friends and had a great time taking in the activities, which included games, crafts, music, entertainment, and of course food, with everyone dressed in period pieces. There were also demonstrations of medieval riding skills, musicians playing medieval instruments, and a re-enactment of an historic 1334 battle. My favourite memory is of a little boy at the *giochi da tavola* (games table) who said he was *Milanese* (from Milan). He was taking on all comers and had a grin from ear to ear.

Ferragosto is a popular national holiday in Italy. Celebrated every year on August 15, it originates from the time of Emperor Augustus, when the *Feriae Augusti* (the holidays of Augustus) were established to celebrate his victory over Mark Anthony at the Battle of Actium. This day later became a holy day in the Catholic Church, called Assumption Day. August is also the height of Italian vacation season, when Italians like to head to the beach or the mountains. Many businesses close and you will see signs hastily stuck to store windows: *Chiuso per Ferie*.

My first time in Italy during Ferragosto was with my sister. We were staying at a B&B above Merano in South Tyrol. My plan was to walk into town to take in the celebrations. I won't bother with the details, but as sisters will do, we managed to get into a scrap and ended up unhappily going our separate ways. I continued into town but quickly lost interest in the celebrations. On my way home I reached out to my sister. She'd managed to stay on a bus too long and had gotten lost, but luckily the driver got her back on track. She ended up at a Bavarian-looking restaurant near our B&B, which is where I found her comforting herself with a beer, or two. We were both glad to be back together and happy to move on. And the restaurant proved to be an upbeat spot, with live music and dancing on the outdoor patio. We sat on the sidelines, taking it in as we savoured our pizza and drinks. And while it was not quite the Ferragosto I had envisioned, everything worked out in the end.

I've seen several Italian weddings from a distance and always wanted to experience one myself. Then, one summer, I got my chance. Italian friends were going back to Trieste, the capital city of the region of Friuli Venezia Giulia, to get married, and we were invited. Tucked up in the northeastern corner of Italy, the region has changed hands multiple times over its history, coming under the control of formidable rulers such as Julius Caesar, Charlemagne, and Napoleon. The result is a region steeped in cultural diversity that truly reflects the history of its people. Friuli is one of the five regions in Italy given special status to help protect its linguistic and cultural heritage.

The population of Trieste is an ethnic mix of its neighbours, including Venice, Austria, and Slovenia, that sets it apart from the rest of Italy, offering a unique blend of Italian and European styles. Once an influential and powerful centre under the

Austro-Hungarian Empire, Trieste was a strategic seaport, trade hub, and shipbuilding centre. By the twentieth century it was a thriving metropolis, its streets lined with Viennese architecture and its coffeehouse clientele including writers and philosophers such as James Joyce, Italo Svevo, and Sigmund Freud.

I was super excited—for our friends, of course, and at the idea of being a guest at an Italian wedding *in Italia*. And from start to finish it did not disappoint.

The ceremony was held in Trieste's ornate Municipio (city hall) building, stretching along much of the sea-facing side of Piazza Unità d'Italia. The former palaces and other attractive structures surrounding the enormous Piazza (said to be the largest sea-facing square in Europe) are some of Trieste's most impressive buildings. They are elegant examples of imperial Austrian architecture, akin to those you would find in Vienna and reflective of Trieste's history. The Piazza's other distinctive feature is its location, open to the Adriatic Sea along one full side. This openness affords one an expansive view of the Piazza that heightens the sense of grandeur. And at night, when the square is illuminated, it is arguably even more beautiful.

Piazza Unità d'Italia.

The bride and groom celebrating in the Piazza.

Everyone gathered to congratulate the newlyweds, then boarded a ferry organised by the couple to transport guests across the Gulf of Trieste to the majestic nineteenth century Miramare Castle. The cream-coloured castle was once the home of Maximilian. He was the younger brother of Franz Joseph I, the beloved leader of the Austrian Empire and then the Austro-Hungarian Empire. Sipping prosecco, we enjoyed a scenic cruise across the bay. Off the ferry, we walked through the castle's elegant garden, renowned for its exotic trees, and on to a seaside restaurant for the reception.

It was a wonderful event that far exceeded my expectations. I have many sweet memories: the excitement as our friends entered the Piazza to streams of confetti; the unique mode of transporting guests to the reception; the unusual location of the restaurant, carved into the side of the cliff; the tranquil sea view as the sun was setting; the delicious food, which focused on local fish and seafood; music and dancing that was both traditional and modern to satisfy all tastes; and a party that continued well into the night. The upbeat party mood was further enhanced by a huge bottle of rum the groom had placed on our table, knowing that it would go over well with the Canadian contingent. While the Italian guests enjoyed their wine and digestives, our table had no difficulty finishing off the bottle, perhaps even two if I'm not mistaken.

My funniest memory was meeting one of the groom's friends, a charismatic young man with a captivating smile. He spoke a little English and I think reached out to our table because we were a small group of English-speaking Canadians. As the evening wore on, his English rapidly deteriorated in proportion to his alcohol consumption, to the point where nothing other than laughter was understood. Some of his friends offered to take him 'off our hands', but he resisted, wanting to continue to connect. It was very endearing and helped forge a connection between the Canadians and the Italians that made us truly feel a part of the group, despite the language barriers.

Another ritual that can't go unmentioned is the daily routine of *gli uomini* (men) playing cards in the park. My best recollection of this is from Bari. Out for a walk, we came across a park full of men of various ages occupying pretty much every available table, with others huddled over them. Everyone was heavily involved in the games being played among the seated players. Gord stood behind one of the tables, to check things out, and we both had to laugh. He was a foot taller than most of them. They too found it funny and humoured me with a photograph.

Gord watching men playing cards in the park.

Like other aspects of what I've referred to as Italy's 'life in the piazza', sagre are a ritualistic slice of Italian life, where you can eat and drink and celebrate with locals, learn about their traditions, and feel their pride. In addition to markets, I now also look for sagre as part of my trip planning. If you're going to visit a town, why not do it when the market is on and there's a party in the streets? Especially in centres that are off the beaten path for tourists, you're likely to have a more authentic experience. Throw in a break for aperitivo and an evening passeggiata, and you will feel like a local in no time.

In concluding here, I want to mention a research finding of interest in the context of rituals and traditions, suggesting that those who place a higher value on tradition also report higher levels of life satisfaction. I was intrigued by this because it seemed to offer tangible evidence to support my intangible emotional connection to a country steeped in tradition.

CHAPTER 10

Vuoi un Caffè – Coffee?

*The caffè with a poor appearance but full of local people
is the best place to enjoy the local specialties and a good
coffee (but not American coffee please).*
—The Dolomites Mountain Guide (Roberto)

Believed to have originated in the Arab world, coffee had been introduced to much of the globe by the seventeenth century and rapidly became a significant part of social life everywhere. Coffeehouses became hubs for intellectual discussion as well as social interaction, and the tradition has clearly flourished.

While mulling over some of the concepts I'd been reading about relating to the human need for social interaction, connection, and a sense of belonging (which strangely seemed to be coming at me from multiple directions), and how they might be related to my infatuation with Italy, I clicked on a taping of Oprah's *Super Soul Sunday*. Her discussion was with Howard Schultz, of Starbuck fame. Mr. Shultz spoke of a trip to Italy in the mid-1980s that changed his life. Recall that this was well before $4 lattes and coffee shops on every other street corner. He recounted the 'romance and theatre' of Italian cafes, where locals would come in as part of their daily routine. As Schultz visited expresso bars throughout Milan and Verona, he said he was 'struck by the power that savouring a simple cup of coffee can have to connect people and create community among them'. It was at the centre of conversation; 'a social experience infused with passion and ritual'.

Anyone who has spent time in Italy will be familiar with this time-honoured ritual, which often involves an espresso or cappuccino, sometimes along with a napkin-wrapped cornetto, while standing at the bar counter chatting with the barista and others. You can expect to see the same locals every day, usually drinking the same coffee as well—*espresso corto, lungo, macchiato,* whatever their preference. For Italians, coffee is much more than just a way to wake up your day. It's a cultural norm, a social routine full of its own rituals.

Schultz returned home to the United States and immediately began looking for a way to replicate the intoxicating atmosphere he had encountered in Italy, an experience that he truly felt could enrich people's lives. Schultz said he was looking to create community and an opportunity for real human connection, and after his experience in Italian coffee shops he was convinced he could do it over a cup of coffee. As he explains in his book:

> Valuing personal connections at a time when so many people sit alone in front of screens, aspiring to build human relationships in an age when so many issues polarize so many are honorable pursuits at the core of who we set out to be.

This statement seems even more relevant today, as I write during the most devastating pandemic that we are likely to see in our lifetime. COVID-19 has stripped us of any sense of normalcy, of our routines, our daily connections with people at work, our friends, our family. We feel isolated, sad that we can't participate in something as simple as going to the local coffee shop to meet up with friends, at least not in the carefree way we used to. Yet, as stripped down as we may feel, people have found ways to reach out and connect, and none more so than the Italians, who were among the earliest and hardest hit.

First, we heard about Italians crowding onto their balconies to sing the National Anthem every evening before pandemic updates were broadcast nationwide. Then it was musicians and singers, professional or not made no difference. They would play and sing traditional songs from their balconies and in the streets, to entertain neighbours and to give each other a little reprieve from the harsh reality that had everyone in lockdown. 'A moment of joy in a moment of anxiety', as one woman put it.

One such gesture of solidarity caught my eye. A *caffè sospeso*, or 'pending coffee', is a coffee paid for in advance as an anonymous act of charity. This tradition began years ago in working-class cafes of Naples, where someone who had experienced good luck would pay for an extra cup of coffee for someone less fortunate. During the pandemic a similar food initiative, labelled *spesa sospesa* was first championed in Milan. Free food was initially delivered in some of the hardest hit areas of Porta Romana, but soon spread elsewhere. In other cities people were asked to buy extra groceries for those in need, much the way we might donate items to the local food bank. The intention behind such initiatives is: *Chi può metta; chi non può prenda*—Those who can, should give; those who can't, should take.

As devastating as the pandemic circumstances may be, they have given us an opportunity to slow down and look back, through the rear-view mirror. We have time to reflect on some of the simple pleasures we may have taken for granted, as well as the pervasive isolation many are feeling due to the lack of face-to-face social interaction. And perhaps, upon reflection, we may begin to fully appreciate how essential these simple rituals are to our emotional well-being. How we are all 'wired for connection'; how face-to-face contact can make us healthier and happier; how intimate social contact is a 'fundamental human need'. While

Italy has been helping me see this for years, the pandemic has perhaps helped bring these thoughts into even greater focus.

I can't describe this sense of loss any better than through the words of an Italian friend who I met on a cruise ship years ago. Matteo worked as a professional barista and sales representative for a major Italian coffee company for many years, and recently pursued his passion—opening his own cafe in his hometown of Chieri, just outside of Turin. As the pandemic ravaged northern Italy, he wrote this passage, which I translated from his Italian. It references a piano performance called 'River Flows in You':

> I was moved to tears as I listened to this song and I am not ashamed to admit it. And you know why? You know who I was thinking about? It was you, my clients. I am your barista and I miss our daily chats. I miss your little habits, even the most annoying ones. I miss your smiles. I miss listening to you share your frustrations about everyday life. I miss joking with you and serving you. Without you, a piece of my heart is empty. I hope we can see each other again very soon because you are not simply customers. You are a part of my life and I miss you.

The cafe where he worked was his home away from home, his customers like family. I see it also as a microcosm of the Italian way of life. The ebb and flow of life plays out in his cafe just as it plays out in the streets and the homes of Italians everywhere. And the loss he is describing, because he can no longer see and serve his customers, is the loss we are all feeling.

Matteo shared another story about life behind the coffee counter, posted to his friends and colleagues several months prior to the pandemic. He wrote about how he is there to make their day better in any way he can, not just with a good cup of coffee;

and how, unfortunately, this can at times be taken for granted. Matteo talked about how beautiful work is for those behind the counter, about feeling like a hero for his customers. He sees their work as much more than just making drinks and sandwiches. To him, 'It is about listening, understanding, offering suggestions where possible'. What really matters 'is the love you put into your work, and how much love you can share with your customers, through a simple smile, calling them by their name.' He was saddened because at times he felt that 'the magic fades', as clients perhaps are too distracted or busy to stop and chat, to connect. He was writing to tell his customers that he wanted to be their hero. 'I would like to add value to your day, and in return I hope we will be appreciated for the effort we take and the subtle differences we can make, even from behind a counter.'

My heart hears what he is saying. It understands the lesson— that each of us has the capacity to profoundly impact the lives of others, even by something as simple as a cup of coffee. The daily dance in Matteo's cafe demonstrates how connected we all are, how we depend on each other, and how important it is to remind ourselves of that.

Although it took some time, Starbucks was the result of Schultz's coffee shop encounters in Italy. Here I must add an editorial comment. To be frank, while the vision may have evolved from the vibrancy Schultz experienced in Italian cafes, I'm not convinced his efforts hit the mark—perhaps like American city squares that, on the surface, resemble their Italian counterparts but lack the substance. You'll be cheerfully greeted and perhaps become acquainted with some of the regulars. But there are too many customers using headphones and technology, disconnecting from those around them rather than connecting, to conclude that the model exactly aligns with the vision.

It also appears that, even before COVID-19 the Starbuck's business model had been moving further from the Italian experience Schultz was captivated by, shifting to more drive-thru and mobile app pick-up locations. And this shift is only accelerating as the world navigates the pandemic and beyond. For now, I still prefer Matteo's version of a cafe, and if I need to go to Italy to find it, so be it.

I haven't had the pleasure of visiting Matteo behind his new coffee bar, but I am happy to say that I have experienced the same emotions elsewhere. La Piccola Caffetteria is the first spot that comes to mind—a tiny coffee shop hugging a corner of Fondi's main piazza, operated by Marta and her brothers. While inside there is barely room for a handful of customers to congregate around the bar counter, the cafe extends outside like a dining table with leaves added to accommodate more guests. There is also an area that can be enclosed in heavy plastic to shield customers against the rain. I know the value of this space well; I have huddled in the middle of it, laughing at the torrential downpour that caught us off guard. On other days, large, cantilevered umbrellas provide shade from the sun.

Filomena and Marta at La Piccola Caffetteria.

For Joe and Fil, the cafe is an extension of their home while in Fondi. You can find them enjoying life here most mornings, and again in the afternoon. Marta is like family at this point. Always with a beautiful smile and a wave, she seems to know everyone's name. She is a special person who shines light and laughter wherever she goes. I can say the same about Filomena, and La Piccola Caffetteria is an especially inviting place to be with these two ladies around.

I should note that in Italy if you order a coffee you will get espresso. The term technically refers to the steam-driven process by which coffee is prepared, a process the Italians introduced to the world in the nineteenth century. In kitchens across Italy, you will find various sizes of *caffettiere* (stove-top espresso coffee makers). The bottom is filled with water, coffee then added to the metal filter above, and a tightly sealed empty portion sits above that. Placed on the stove, the heat creates steam and pressure that forces the water up through the coffee grounds, ending up as espresso in the top section.

This method differs from drip coffee, where hot water drips from above, through the grounds and filter into the pot below. Interestingly, because the amount of caffeine is proportional to the brewing time, an espresso contains less caffeine than filtered coffee, despite its intensive taste and appearance.

If you want something other than espresso you ask for it specifically—cappuccino (espresso with a little milk and more foam), caffè latte (espresso with mostly hot milk), caffè macchiato ('dirty coffee', so with just a splash of hot milk), or as my friend Filomena likes, *un macchiato lungo, con un po' di schiuma*. And what exactly is that? It's a shot of espresso, run long with a little extra hot water, with a dollop of foam on top. In fact, because Fil is such a regular, her 'usual' is now called the 'Filomena' for short! Even though my usual is more likely to be an *Americano con latte caldo al parte* (espresso and hot water with a little steamed milk on the side), I do like to order a 'Filomena' occasionally, just for fun, or at least until I'm enough of a regular to have a drink named after me.

While the 'Filomena' may be specific to the Piccola Caffetteria, the friendly, welcoming atmosphere is not, as we have seen from Matteo's description of the cafe where he worked. Other cafes come to mind as well, like the friendly owner of a cafe in Casale who offered to keep an eye on my bike when I didn't have a lock, and the cafe in the tiny train station in even smaller Zollino (Apulia), where I was complimented on my choppy effort to speak Italian as I lingered over my cappuccino.

In the Tuscan town of Pienza, I learned about the man behind the counter who, like Matteo, was a professional barista, having made coffee his career for over 25 years. As with professional gelato makers, the idea that people make a career out of coffee service was not something that had previously occurred to me. My impression had been that baristas are often working to put themselves through school or to supplement a household income. But after talking to this man, and after reading Matteo's perspective from behind *il banco*, I now have a different understanding of the art of coffee, and the passion behind the counter.

I'm sorry to say that my coffee rituals will instantly give my non-resident status away. I can't drink coffee without milk, no matter what time of day, and I like a big mug of coffee that will last longer than the time it takes to knock back a shot of espresso.

During my time at La Casaccia, for example, my ritual was to wake early and head to the kitchen to make myself an Americano-sized coffee (my apologies to the Dolomites Mountain Guide). I started with espresso, made in a stove-top caffettiera, and added *orzo* (a caffeine-free beverage made from roasted barley) and hot milk. I would then traipse back to my room to savour it while doing some reading. Once noise began to seep from the kitchen, I'd head back, start another pot of coffee, and help with breakfast. Elena (owner of La Casaccia with her husband Giovanni) usually prepared a home-made muesli with cultured yogurt, various seeds that she ground every morning, in-season fruit, and freshly squeezed lemon juice. It took some work but was about as healthy as you can get. This filling breakfast usually kept me going for most of the morning, except when we worked until 2 p.m. and it seemed lunch would never come.

Back to the coffee—when I say 'pot' I need to put it in perspective. At La Casaccia, one small caffettiera was shared by up to five of us at times. It was not my idea of a morning coffee, but since I'd satisfied my craving earlier, I was good to go. One exception was at lunch, when Giovanni might dig out the gelato to quench his insatiable *dente dolce* (sweet tooth). We'd make a big pot of espresso and then enjoy *un affogato,* gelato covered in warm espresso. If Giovanni was in a good mood, which he always was, the gelato flowed even more than the coffee. I always enjoyed lingering over lunch in the courtyard, but it was even sweeter when finished off this way.

On a related note, I smile recalling how the caffettiera we used for five or six *affogati* was the same size pot I used to make morning coffee for a B&B guest. He drank the full pot himself, and then asked for a second. That was a lot of coffee, even for me; but like the Italians, we all have our rituals.

Of course, meeting for coffee is a common activity for many of us in North America as well (at least pre-pandemic). But there are differences. In so many cases, people are on their laptops or mobile devices, headphones on, working, checking social media, seemingly unaware of the strangers around them. Sure, many people carry their cell phone in Italy, perhaps even more so than North America if that is possible. But in Italy I sensed people were there with the desire to engage with others, not buried in technology and oblivious to what is going on around them. The fact that coffee is traditionally a daily ritual of many elderly in Italy may also be a factor in this regard.

That said, I don't want to diminish the coffee culture that is thriving around the world. Many people have rituals they have practised religiously, and hopefully will be able to continue to do so as the world sorts out the pandemic. These rituals may look different than the Italian traditions I've mentioned, but the intent is there. In Canada's northern climate, some involve walking the shopping malls and then congregating around a coffee shop in the food court; or local farmers meeting at a spot in town where coffee is cheap and refills free. The quality of the coffee is secondary to the time spent socializing.

I'm smiling as I think of the pre-pandemic rituals of a couple of friends. In one case, a friend liked to stop for a coffee while out cycling. However, unlike most Italians, her ritual was to search out different cafes to visit each time. On the other hand, if I wanted to find my retired Italian friend, Joe, I pretty much knew that in the early afternoon I could just head down to *il bar* in Little Italy and he would be sitting there chatting with friends. I can also think of a 'coffee shop crowd' I know who became friends over time as they shared the start of their day at the same coffee shop. And like my Italian friends, they found their own ways to adapt during the pandemic, even if it meant enjoying a take-out coffee in a parking lot and visiting through their car windows.

Matteo.

While the pandemic has severely altered our habits as they relate to coffee, my hope is that each of us is able to find safe alternatives that feed our soul as well as our coffee cravings.

CHAPTER 11

Tutto con Passione –
Everything with Passion

It's a helluva start being able to recognize what makes you happy.

—Lucille Ball

In her book, *La Passione*, Dianne Hales examines why so many of us fall in love with Italy and the Italian lifestyle. She also quotes a woman as saying, 'We do not choose our passion. Passion chooses us.' I could not agree more.

When it comes to passion, I must tell you about two incredibly special men, both named Giovanni. The first you will learn about here, the second Giovanni in the next chapter.

With the passion and dedication of an Italian football fan, Giovanni#1 oversees his family's wine and olive oil operation in the Chianti wine district of Tuscany. Resting on a hilltop overlooking the gentle Tuscan landscape, the agriturismo is appropriately called Il Colle (The Hill). It consists of several superbly restored villas surrounded by fields of Giovanni's beloved vineyards and olive trees. As the sun sets, the lights of Florence sparkle in the distance. We spent four relaxing nights here with friends, using the B&B as our base to tour the medieval cities of Florence and Siena, and towns along the scenic Strada del Vino (Wine Route) such as Greve, Panzano, and Castellina. This fertile region was settled well before the Etruscans arrived in the eighth century BC. Today it offers a sense of tranquility that belies a history that was not always as peaceful.

For example, the ancient walls of Castellina were rebuilt and reinforced each time the town was destroyed during battles between the powerful city-states of Siena and Florence. Remnants of medieval fortifications remain, including the castle (called the Rocca), which has 360-degree views from atop its massive fourteenth-century tower, a perfect lookout then and now. Panzano is a charming village between Greve and Castellina and it too was constantly under siege by one or other of the feuding powers. After wandering around the old town, we stopped in the piazza for a coffee and the owner graciously allowed us to dig into the *schiacciata con fiche* dessert we had purchased elsewhere on our trip. Schiacciata is a traditional Tuscan flatbread where the dough is *schiacciata* (pressed) into the pan and then topped—in our case with glazed fresh figs and walnuts, for a sweeter effect.

This area of Tuscany is renowned for its wine. In fact, Chianti Classico was the first classified wine production area in the history of wine, demarcated in 1716 when the Grand Duke of Tuscany officially recognised its boundaries. The signature black rooster confirms that production of the wine has been regulated by the Consorzio Vino Chianti Classico (Chianti Classico Wine Consortium). A bottle's DOCG (Denomination of Origin Controlled and Guaranteed) certification attests to the vintage's superior quality. To obtain this label, very strict standards must be met related to factors such as the production process, yields, alcohol content, aging, and taste. Other well-known Italian wines that have garnered a DOCG designation include Barolo, Brunello di Montalcino, and Amarone della Valpolicella.

With the help of a few employees, Giovanni produces Chianti Classico and extra virgin olive oil, both labours of love. I spoke with him every morning as he offered us coffee on the terrace outside his little office. *Cento percento Arabica!* he would exclaim, meaning 'the best'. The office space was filled with wine bottles, various incarnations of the symbolic Chianti rooster, and cards from past guests who, like us, appreciated Giovanni and all that Il Colle had to offer. He had a contagious smile and a zest for life like I'm not sure I've seen before. Despite being busy with the grape harvest, he seemed to have all the time in the world for guests. I loved practising my Italian with him and listening to him talk about his work, his family, the Tuscan way of life.

I'm going on about Giovanni because that zest for life is at the core of my love for Italy. He lived nearby, with his grandfather in an apartment beside him, and his mother above. Family was everything. He also explained that the three classic features of the landscape Tuscans treasure most are their grape vines, their olive trees, and their cypress trees. I could certainly see why.

An icon of rural Tuscany, Italian cypresses are tall, slender, long living trees that picturesquely dot the landscape. Considered a symbol of eternal life and used in many sacred sites, they may have been introduced to Italy by the Etruscans. The wood is rich in fragrant oils, used for their therapeutic properties. Today you will see these elegant trees planted in an orderly fashion around churches and cemeteries, or lining long drives leading to country estates. Despite being tolerant to heavy wind (they are often planted as windbreaks), they also have the advantage of shallow roots, so they do not dig up the ground.

More than anything, I remember how often Giovanni would exclaim to me, *Passione Susan, tutto con passione!* Everything with passion! His passion became my passion, and he left an enduring impression that continues to flavour Italy for me. I found other examples of Italians demonstrating their passion for everything from church to calcio, and the more I saw of their passion for life the more mine grew.

Giovanni during a wine and olive oil
tasting at Agriturismo Il Colle.

La Chiesa – Church

Present in Italy since the first century, Christianity was legalised by Constantine's Edict of Milan in 313 AD, which gave religious liberty to people of all faiths and beliefs. It was recognised as the official religion of the Roman Empire by an edict of Emperor Theodosius in 380 AD. Prior to this, Roman authorities considered Christianity a superstition and even a form of rebellion against the Empire and its way of life. Christians were persecuted and often imprisoned for preaching their religious beliefs, the apostles Peter and Paul eventually martyred in Rome for it.

Once it was officially recognised, however, Christianity became the predominant unifying force across Europe, and bishops replaced emperors in positions of leadership and power. While the church's power and influence declined after the high point of the Middle Ages, and there is much debate about the role of religion in modern Italy, it is hard to deny that it has permeated every aspect of life, from art and architecture to health care and education.

According to available data, church attendance remains high in comparison to the average of other Western European countries. Together with family, the church remains at the heart of Italian life, even if fewer Italians are actively practising their religion. As Hales puts it, 'Although religious practices are fading, Italians' love of God and their saints endures.'

Churches themselves are a focal part of the landscape of every urban centre, with bells in the campanile chiming regularly to remind us of their presence. The traditions of life—baptisms, weddings, and funerals—all play out in the church, with other religious traditions taking place in the streets. References to Padre Pio, the revered saint of Pietrelcina (Campania), are everywhere, and his feast day is celebrated throughout Italy. I recall Italian friends passing on their weekly dinner-dance evening to attend ceremonies honouring Padre Pio. I also remember seeing Joe's elderly aunts in Fondi passing by regularly, on their way to daily prayer. Even death is shared in a public way, with large posters displayed throughout town to remember those who have passed, community connections being made even in death.

Taking a different perceptive, the Dolomites Mountain Guide, who clearly has a good sense of humour, had this to say about religion:

> In Italy coexists three religions in good [h]armony; the football, the aperitif, and in last position the Christian religion. Football and Christian religion are practiced on Sunday. The aperitif every day. In any case, Italy is traditionally a Catholic country where it is better you will have a devotion and

respect for the church. Alternatively, you can be burnt near the column of the main square (but not on Sunday during the local football match or before aperitif time).

Whether they practise their faith or not, Italians can be sticklers when it comes to respecting religious traditions and the sanctity of their holy sites. I found no exception at the Benedictine Monastery above Monte Cassino (Lazio). While my shoulders were covered, my skirt was insufficiently modest by traditional standards. Fortunately, I remembered the rules just before getting to the gate and quickly implemented my favourite trick—pulling my skirt down below my hips and untucking my shirt so it hung over the top of my sagging waist band, thus at least offering the appearance of modesty. It worked! We were ushered in without a second glance.

I was not as lucky a second time, when we wanted to climb the campanile at St. Peter's Basilica in Rome. Before having a chance to put my stunt into action, I looked up to see the deadpan expression of a security guard who was wagging his finger at me. *No! No! No!* I laid on my best Italian, attitude and all, and tried to negotiate, pulling my skirt down to show him how respectful it was. I pointed to a woman who had just descended the tower steps with a dress no longer than my skirt. Still the wagging finger. Just as I felt I'd lost the battle, my adversary waved me off to a second guard. It was perhaps out of exhaustion, though we suspected his *machismo* might have been at play—how could he let this woman wear him down? Following a look of indignation, I was gestured on. Success. And in Italian no less! I was pleased with myself, even if I was arguing with church authorities, in a foreign country and a foreign language.

Without stopping to count, I can safely say I've been in many of the most famous churches across Italy. And while their beauty and grace are undeniable, displaying some of the finest art and architecture Italy has to offer, it is the experiences surrounding my visits that made some extra special.

With my dad, and the pigeons, in Piazza del Duomo, Milan (1971).

The cathedral in Milan is memorable for a few reasons. Although I'd been to this northern city as a child, it was close to a half century before I returned. In this dated picture of me and my dad standing in the middle of Piazza del Duomo, the cathedral is our backdrop. The ploy of photographers (then and now) was to offer tourists kernels of corn to attract some of the square's many pigeons, and then snap pictures they hoped to sell. Although my dad did end up buying the pictures, there was no smile on my face—I remember being afraid of the birds as they hopped onto my hand in a feeding frenzy. When I returned as an adult, the pigeons were my friends and I had fun trying to replicate the shot from my childhood.

Another church that stands out despite its small size is Sansevero Chapel in Naples. The entrance fee seemed steep for such a small chapel but seeing Guiseppe Sanmartino's marble sculpture of the Veiled Christ was beyond price. I was glad we hadn't given up in frustration after roaming the narrow streets of this ancient neighbourhood before finally locating the Baroque chapel, tucked away on a small side street. Inside,

I remember staring in awe, wondering how the veil, delicately carved from the same block of marble as the body of Christ beneath it, could seem so real, as if a translucent shroud was hanging over the lifeless body. You do not have to be religious to appreciate this masterpiece.

Speaking of Naples reminds me of a visit to its cathedral, Duomo di Napoli. While my girlfriend and I toured the church, our counterparts preferred to hang out on the church steps, beverage of choice in hand. Their location proved to be a perfect spot for a local side show—a young couple amorously comingling on the steps below them that far outshone their own lack of reverence. But I digress.

Even though it is well outside Vatican City, the Basilica of San Giovanni in Laterano (not St. Peter's Basilica) is the official Cathedral of Rome and seat of the Bishop of Rome, the Pope. Built in the fourth century, it is believed to be one of the first Catholic churches in the city. Standing beside the Basilica are the Scala Santa—said to be the steps Jesus climbed on the way to his trial in Jerusalem and later transported to Rome. I remember asking two nuns who were sitting in front of the Basilica, *Mi scusi. Dove posso trovare le Scala Santa?* (Where can I find the Holy Stairs, please?) While the answer turned out to be more than obvious as soon as I asked, I received a warm smile as one nun pointed across the piazza. I understand from my friend Joe that as a young boy, and much to his mother's surprise, he decided to climb the stairs on his knees, the only means one is allowed to ascend the holy steps. We had no plans to do the same, but it was humbling to see others expressing their faith in this way.

I have fond memories of visiting a few of Rome's earliest Christian churches with my mom. In addition to the well-known Basilica di San Pietro (St. Peter's Basilica), Santa Maria Maggiore, and Santa Maria in Trastevere, we visited the lesser known Santa Pudenziana (considered the oldest place of Christian worship in Rome), Santa Prassede (built to house relics of two female saints who were murdered for providing Christian burials for early martyrs, in defiance of Roman law), and Sant'Agnese Fuori le Mura (built in the seventh century over second-century catacombs of the martyr Saint Agnes). It was special visiting these sites together because they were so meaningful to my mom and her faith. I also appreciated having my own guide, which made the visits considerably more interesting as she explained the Bible stories behind the mosaics and paintings.

With my mom in Rome.

The hilltop Abbey of Monte Cassino, one of the oldest in Europe, was founded by Saint Benedict in 529. It was destroyed and rebuilt several times over history. The last major destruction occurred during World War II in an ill-fated effort by the Allies to dislodge a German stronghold they believed was entrenched atop this strategic location. The 1944 Battle of Monte Cassino was a turning point in the war, but at incredible cost. More than 55,000 Allied troops were killed, including many Polish soldiers now buried in a dedicated Polish cemetery below. I've been here several times, a panoramic spot on a rocky hill about 130 km south of Rome, but my memories are as much of the stories I learned as the scenery.

Driving from Fondi on a day trip once, we crossed a small bridge in the middle of Pontecorvo. Peter, one of the friends we were travelling with, perked up and asked, 'Are we in Pontecorvo? My dad was stationed here.' He explained that his father had been involved in logistics, secretly advancing ahead of the Allied forces and sending back coordinates on the location of German artillery targets. We followed up our subsequent visit to the monastery with a tour of the nearby War Museum. The area had experienced some of the worst fighting and greatest losses (including many Canadian soldiers) during the Allied forces' efforts to free Italy from the occupying German army. But it was also where key battles were won.

Discussion of Monte Cassino and the Second World War also reminded me of stories that Joe told of his father, Luigi. Italy had been led into the war by the Fascist government of Benito Mussolini, who had formed an alliance with Germany in 1936. After Mussolini's government collapsed towards the end of the war, Italy did an about-face and sided with the Allies. This left hundreds of thousands of Italian troops in limbo, now enemies of the Germans they had been fighting alongside.

Luigi was one of them. He'd been stationed at an Italian military airport in Apulia when the news was broadcast, at which point he and others began their long trek home. About 300 km into their walk, the soldiers were stopped near Cassino by the Allied forces. Here they were commandeered to assist the Americans with the gruesome task of removing and burying soldiers who had been killed in the conflict. Eventually Luigi was released to continue his journey home, with a discharge letter in hand lest he be stopped again. I believe Joe still has that letter.

Of the churches I've seen, my favourite remains the Madonna del Miracolo, a tiny stone church just up the hill from Fondi. I hike up this stretch of road almost every morning when I'm in Fondi and always stick my head through the door of the chapel on my way. I don't think I've ever seen anyone in it, but the door is always open, which I take as a sign to come on in, say a little thank-you for the many blessings in my life, and continue along my way. No matter my mood when I get there, I always walk away feeling lighter.

Calcio – Football/Soccer

I started playing soccer after competing extensively for many years as a volleyball player and then a rower. I had no idea how tough this 'non-contact' sport was going to be on my body, but I was hooked before I figured that out. While I ended up with more injuries than I could have imagined, I wouldn't have changed that decision. It introduced me to ladies I'm blessed to call friends today, and to my group of Italian friends, for which I will always be thankful. I'm quite certain that it also had a great deal to do with my ongoing obsession with Italy.

An early soccer experience that helped reinforce my infatuation with Italy occurred during a trip to the World Cup in Germany, way back in 2006. The Italian connection came when my soccer friend and I continued our travels to Switzerland, and from there a quick trip south into Lombardy. Our accommodations at a local hostel in Como were not particularly memorable, but it was here that I saw first-hand the Italian passion for calcio and for their beloved Azzurri (the nickname of Italy's national team).

We found a spot in a cafe along the lakeshore that was showing a must-win game for Italy on a large screen they had set up under a big tent. What I remember most is the excitement exuding from local fans who were glued to the screen. Italy won (in extra time on a controversial call as I recall) following which, absolute craziness erupted: everyone pouring into the streets; fans racing their Vespas along the lakeshore, hollering and waving their Italian *bandiere* (flags) behind them; car horns honking. Noticing the clarity of these memories as I look back, the experience of being in the midst of their celebrations obviously left an impression.

Whether it was the excitement of the win, or just business as usual for males in Italy at that time, I can't help smiling when I recall an incident with a local that occurred after the game. While walking back to our car, a man offered a smile as we passed by. I smiled back. The next thing I knew there was a little slip of paper pressed into my hand. Stopping to look at it, I wasn't sure if I should be offended or amused. It was his name and phone number. *Ma che cazz'?* WTF? Is a smile all it takes for someone to assume you're interested in them? Fine, perhaps, if I was by myself, or just with a girlfriend. But for all he knew my brother, who was also with us, could have been my husband. Apparently, that was irrelevant.

Two equally memorable experiences involving Italy's love of calcio occurred the following year. At one point on our trip, we visited a small hill town in Tuscany called San Casciono dei Bagni, the closest town to the villa we had rented with friends. We had plans to meet up for pizza on our last night together, but I was also looking forward to watching the Champions League final; Italy's AC Milan was playing Liverpool. I'd scouted around the quiet town that afternoon and was told that the only public place we would find a television on Sunday was the local Seniors' Centre. Excusing myself after dinner, I headed off to check it out.

I was directed upstairs when I got there, where I found a group of anziani glued to the television set—at least until this *alta bionda* walked in. As you can imagine, as a tall blond female I did not exactly fit in, but the men quickly returned their attention to the game as I sat quietly in the back. Then Italy scored! I remember the scene as if it were yesterday. One of the older men jumped up from his seat, arms in the air, and yelled *Birra!* He bought a round for everyone. Gord and a couple of our friends joined me shortly after this outburst and his kind offer was extended to them as well.

When the game was over, we learned that our new friend was the *macellaio* (butcher) in town. He invited us to visit him at his shop the next day, which we did with pleasure. After a chat in my then utterly broken Italian, he sent us on our way with an armload of sausages. On a sombre note, several years later when Gord and I were in the area again, we made a point of looking up our friend, the butcher. Sadly, we learned that he was at the hospital, sitting with his dying wife.

Later during that same trip, while we were in the southern region of Campania with my brother, we found the streets of Naples decked out in team Napoli flags and colours. It was a wet soccer Sunday, but the rain had not dampened the spirits of a boy we met standing beside the *forno al legno* (wood-burning oven) in his father's pizzeria, sporting his team paraphernalia as a proud Napoli fan.

It was not just any game that day. If Napoli won or tied the match, their team would be promoted to Serie A, calcio's equivalent of the big leagues. Beaming from ear to ear, the boy could barely contain his excitement. I only wish I could have seen him after the game. Later in the day, while exploring the Royal Palace and Piazza del Plebiscito in central Naples, we saw barricades going up, along with more banners and flags. I knew instantly that Napoli was heading to Serie A, and there would be huge celebrations in the streets.

Musing over comments from the Dolomites Mountain Guide on the tension between calcio and religion, I understood exactly what he was talking about on at least one occasion. I was in Rome with friends; two of the three were soccer teammates. Because it was Sunday and the Pope was giving mass, St. Peter's was closed to visitors until 1 p.m. As an alternative, we opted for a hop-on hop-off bus tour, which offered a quick and easy introduction to Rome's major attractions.

Later, back at St. Peter's Square, diverging interests came into play. Now that the Basilica was open for visitors, the line-up was longer than ever, and we were butting up against the important stuff: Italy was scheduled to play in a preliminary round of another World Cup. Because I'd been to St. Peter's several times before, the urge to go again was not as compelling for me. But for our non-soccer friend who had never been to Italy, the Basilica was a must—and rightly so. Religious or not, few tourists go to Rome without a visit to St. Peter's, and since we only had one day, it was now or never. While the other two had also never been to Italy before, their priorities were clear—calcio and vino! Fair enough. According to the Dolomites Mountain Guide, they were the true Italians.

La Musica – Music

As a child I did not last long on the violin my dad bought me, hoping I'd learn some Béla Bartók, his favourite composer. That said, I do enjoy music, my eclectic tastes likely budding from my mom playing everything from classical music on the piano to Bob Dylan and Leonard Cohen records, my brother's tastes ranging from the Beatles to Led Zeppelin, and my sister on her clarinet and recorder. I was introduced to Italian music later in life. My younger Italian friends laugh at some of the songs I know, as they tend to be artists from the era of my older friends, but there's no accounting for taste.

Eros Ramazzotti has been a big star in Italy for years, but I learned about him quite by accident. I was in a local coffee shop in Canada when I heard a song that I instantly fell in love with. After inquiring with the barista, I jotted down the peculiar name from the CD cover she showed me and immediately went and bought it. He became a favourite of mine for many years. I discovered another huge Italian pop star, Laura Pausini, through a song she'd recorded in English. And later, on my trips to Italy, I learned more about classic favourites, such as Lucio Battisti and Fiorella Mannoia.

In addition to helping me with my Italian as I worked to sing along, music continued to build my connection with Italy. At times I'm surprised by the emotion some songs elicit, even when I don't understand the words. Andrea Bocelli tops my list. I love his story, his dedication to supporting various causes, and of course, his music. I was lucky to see him in a concert in Canada, but it would be amazing to see him perform live in Italy, ideally in the stunning open-air amphitheatre near his Tuscan hometown, Teatro del Silenzio in Lajatico.

The *tarantella* is perhaps the most recognised form of traditional music in southern Italy. Of pagan origin, it includes folk dances known by different names in different areas, appreciated for their lively tempo and quick steps. Sometimes referred to as the dance of the spider, the vigorous tarantella is said to have originated as an ancient healing ritual for victims of a venomous tarantula bite. More recently, the dance is about love and passion, couples dancing frantically to the rhythm of tambourines and accordions, the women waving their scarves and inviting men to join them.

The *pizzica* is a type of tarantella from the Salento area of Apulia. La Notte della Taranta (Tarantella Night) is a local festival that celebrates this tradition each summer when the towns and villages in Salento come together to host concerts and dances featuring musicians from around the world. Concerts are held throughout the area in July, leading up to the main event in August. While in Salento for my yoga retreat one July, I got a small taste of this music. I wasn't close enough to see the dancing, but as different as it was, I was drawn to the music's rhythm and energy.

One of my favourite Sunday evening activities in Fondi is to join a group of friends at a restaurant, called Al Boschetto, with large dance floors and indoor-outdoor dining. The group meets here every week, with rare exception. Some eat full meals, others just an *antipasto* or a salad and fruit, but all get up and dance. The first time we joined the group was with our Fondi friends, Joe and Fil. I was amused to see everyone line dancing, something more expected with country music in North America. It was a staple for most of the evening, and everyone seemed to know the steps to many different songs.

Maria Pia (a good friend of Joe and Fil's who we had gotten to know) would grab my hand and pull me onto the dance floor when a good song came on ('good' meaning not too fast), or Lucio (her husband) would wave at me to join them. I was useless at first, finding it impossible to follow along when we kept changing direction, but the ladies were encouraging. Maria Pia would say in Italian, 'Stand behind and watch me first, then follow Lucio when we turn.' And Loreta, an adorable friend of theirs, would quietly count steps in Italian beside me and whisper *Gira! Gira!* when it was time to turn. They made these occasions extra special.

Gord and I were invited to join the group one year even when Joe and Fil couldn't make it to Fondi, and everyone made us feel welcome. On a sad note, the evening ended abruptly when a woman collapsed after receiving devastating news about her nephew. Everyone knew the family; it was distressing for all.

In joy and sadness, these evenings are unlike anything we do at home, but I love everything about them, especially the sense of community. No one was left on the sidelines, even the tall *Canadese* who didn't know how to line dance.

While their chosen passions may differ widely, whether wine or music, calcio or the chiesa, the passion I experienced of Italians living their lives to the fullest was definitely part of Italy's appeal for me. These experiences have been tucked away in a library of memories that are central to my love for Italy and a large part of what fuels my desire to keep returning for more.

CHAPTER 12

La Spiaggia – The Beach

You may have the universe if I may have Italy.
—Giuseppe Verdi

With such an extensive coastline, Italy has more than its fair share of beaches. My understanding is that you are never more than a two-hour drive from a beach in Italy. To a land-locked Canadian, this seems a luxury. And Italians do love their beaches. They also have their beach culture down to a fine art. Like their appreciation for food and fashion, it's in their blood.

Although beachgoing may come naturally to Italians, over the years I've discovered a few tricks of the trade that have been helpful for us rookies. For starters, you need to know what beach to go to and when. Like many of us, Italians tend to be creatures of habit and get attached to their favourite location, often reserving their spot at a private beach club for the season. Some places are great for morning walks but get windy in the afternoon—hence the kite surfers we saw, rather than sunbathers, one afternoon on a breezy walk. While some beaches require a steep walk down a rocky path, usually there's a reason people make the effort. Other than by boat, this is the only access to some of Sardinia's most spectacular beaches. There are also lots of rocky beaches, in which case you look for the smoothest one to claim as your 'beach' for the day.

One of my first experiences with a rock beach was on Ponza, the largest of the Pontine Islands, formed from the remains of an extinct volcano. To get there, we boarded a high-speed boat in Terracina (Lazio), and after arriving in Porto Ponza we hopped on a local bus for a short ride north. Here we descended to the emerald-green waters of Piscine Naturali, a beach area named for its natural swimming pools. The rocks were surprisingly smooth, eroded by years of wind and lapping tides. But for someone more accustomed to sandy beaches, lying on the rocks did take some getting used to, as did the lack of elbow room—to be expected during the peak of summer at one of the island's top attractions. That said, we managed to find space to lay our towels and niches in the rocks to balance our umbrellas and enjoyed a lovely afternoon.

Most of my lessons in Italian beach culture are thanks to Joe and Fil, and some of my favourite beach memories are times spent with them. Umbrellas and beach chairs loaded in the trunk of their car, we'd pack sandwiches and fruit for lunch, maybe some biscotti, and lots of water, slip on our beach wear, stop at a nearby shop for Joe's newspaper, and we were off. Where you find long expanses of wide sandy beach, you're likely to find most of it covered by the *ombrelloni* and *lettini* (large umbrellas and sun loungers) of private beach clubs. If you don't want to pay beach club prices, look for a slice of sand with mismatched umbrellas. This is where we peasants go.

The expanse of coast near Fondi is called the Ulysses Riviera after the ancient hero who is said to have spent time here. The Riviera is renowned for its clear waters and fine sand beaches, which garner the prestigious *Bandiera Blu* (Blue Flag) year after year. Joe used to rave about the beaches here, but until I had made my way to every region of Italy, I had no idea just how right he was. In addition to some stunning beaches, the calcareous nature of the rocks along this coast has led to some impressive features, such as Montagna Spaccata (Split Mountain) in Gaeta, Tiberius Cave in Sperlonga, and Grotta delle Capre (Goats' Cave) in Monte Circeo. I have spent memorable days exploring the area, on my own at times, but even more enjoyably with Gord and our friends.

I recall an early adventure with Joe and Fil, trying to find Goats' Cave in the rocky outcrop of Monte Circeo. The area is fascinating, with interesting features such as the still-active Capo Circeo Lighthouse and ruins of an ancient Roman acropolis from the third or fourth century BC. While the headland is quite rocky and steep, the eastern side is low-lying and swampy, remnants of the ancient Pontine Marshes that were reclaimed for agriculture and urban development in the 1920s. This area is separated from the sea by an extensive span of coastal dunes, part of Circeo National Park. After numerous stops to enquire about directions to the grotto (*grotta* in Italian), we finally found the parking area and made our way down a narrow path to the cave. An archaeological find suggests it was inhabited in prehistoric times, and it was later used as a burial ground by the Romans.

Our friends took us to numerous spots along the miles of beach near Fondi. In the earlier years it was often Sant'Anastasia, at the mouth of a canal by the same name. The canal connects Lago di Fondi, a coastal lake of volcanic origin, with the Tyrrhenian Sea. This is where Joe's family would spend their beach days before immigrating to Canada. On other occasions we'd drive to the seaside resort of Sperlonga and walk to the public beach near Tiberius Cave. There are gorgeous long sandy beaches, as well as enticing nooks and crannies, all along the coast. But you need to know where to go, and more importantly, where to park. Joe and Fil showed us where to park without breaking the bank, where to beat the crowds, how to get our umbrella to stay up in the wind, how to keep our clothes out of the sand and, of course, their favourite places *per un caffè*.

Vendors were constantly walking the beach, selling everything from fresh coconut to plastic beach gear. Filomena was always kind, chatting with them and often offering them fruit, which they graciously accepted. Many would get work picking fruit in the fertile plains around Fondi after the beach season. Most were from North Africa; some from further afield, such as Bangladesh. It's a tough life, but most had smiles to share and were always respectful. It seemed as if being treated with respect was even more important to them than the sale, and Fil understood that.

More recently we'd pay to park at a little beach bar called Moorea, happy to support the family-run business. Luigi's older daughter was behind the coffee bar, son Vincenzo helping with the grounds and beach rentals, and dad pitching in wherever needed. On one visit we met little Angelica, the youngest. My goodness, she was indeed a little angel, like her name suggested, and so smart too. She was learning English in school and was able to respond to our questions and translate for her father. She had a mop of blond curls like her brother, and a smile that she clearly got from her dad.

In late summer of the following year, we were at Moorea when Luigi's family had a rare opportunity to relax over lunch. They were eating a type of *panzanella* that an aunt had made, a common dish for using up stale bread. Unlike the tomato-y Tuscan version I was familiar with, this one included cooked onion, *pancetta* (bacon), and chickpeas. Noticing my inquisitive look, Luigi's daughter brought me a plate of my own. It was surprisingly tasty. Luigi said the pancetta and onions added a lot of flavour. When I asked how it was made, I was guided to a nearby picnic table with members of their extended family, including the aunt who had made the dish. After a lively conversation I was given detailed instructions. I'm not sure I'll make it, but I have notes somewhere, just in case.

We also happened to be at Moorea on the last day of the season. Even though the weather was pleasant by our standards, Italians rarely go to the beach after the kids are back at school. They may come for a walk, or for a picnic on weekends, but by the end of September most places have closed. Luigi was melancholy. He said it was hard work being there 10 to 12 hours per day, every day. He was looking forward to some downtime. But in his next breath, before he'd locked the gate for the final time that season, he admitted that already he was missing it. The beach is his life, and his passion.

A favourite memory from Moorea occurred as we were returning from a walk along the beach. Gord noticed Luigi cleaning the sand in front of his place and as is his instinct, picked up a rake to help. They speak different languages, but no words were required. Luigi was astonished that someone would want to help for no reason. But that's Gord—and he did get a cold Moretti out of it.

Gord and Luigi in front of Moorea.

Found along Liguria's rugged coast in northwest Italy, Cinque Terre (the name comes from Ligurian *Çinque Taere*, meaning 'Five Lands') is not necessarily famous for its beaches, but you never know where beautiful experiences will unfold. The area was named a national park in 1999, Italy's first, in recognition of its scenic, agricultural, historic, and cultural value. It includes a group of five ancient fishing communities, each with clusters of multi-coloured houses clinging to steep rocks that tumble straight into the sea. The villages are linked by walking paths that wind along the cliffs, but they are more accessible by trains or boats. Each offers a unique experience.

The local train that runs through the park is included in the price of a park pass. Although it doesn't provide much in the way of views, it is a convenient option for visiting the five villages as one can easily hop on and off at any of the stops. The boats that ply the waters between the villages are a fun alternative, offering wonderful views of the towns from the water, but their schedules are weather-dependent. Because the tiny marinas lack sophisticated docking facilities, services are routinely cancelled if the sea is rough. The hiking paths that link the villages are an exciting choice for those with energy to spare. You can read more about them in Chapter 14.

If you are looking for the best beach town along this portion of the Italian Riviera, head to Monterosso al Mare, the only town with a long sandy beach. You will see a few private beach areas with their colourful ombrelloni on display, but there is public beach space as well.

My memories of *la spiaggia* in this part of Italy are from Vernazza, however. Despite being a busy place, and a challenge to get in the water depending where you find a spot, I was impressed that my elderly mother made her way in for a swim.

Growing up in Scotland, she was used to swimming in the sea, and loved to take advantage of such opportunities.

Recalling her swimming adventure reminded me of a return visit when, after a tough hike from Monterosso, I was ready for a dip of my own. It was short and sweet, but while sitting on the rocks to dry off I noticed the cutest little Italian girl in just her pink swimming briefs. She was excited to get in the water, but also tentative. The rocks were sharp in places and slippery in others. Her father was encouraging without being pushy, letting her feel her way over the moss-covered rocks. Finally finding the perfect entry point, she slid into the cool water with a huge smile on her face. She put a smile on my face as well.

The Ligurian town of Vernazza.

My favourite beach day in Apulia was when a large group from my yoga retreat car-pooled to Grotta della Poesia (Poetry Cave) on the Adriatic coast. Here I experienced beach culture like nothing before. And when I say 'beach day' I mean a full day. We departed after breakfast, and I recall sipping a glass of prosecco at a beachside cafe around 5 p.m. before anyone began thinking about heading home.

Enjoying a glass of prosecco at the beach.

A friendly participant from Rome had packed fruit, and someone else had brought biscotti. That was enough for most of us, but there were also options for more substantial fare if one was so inclined. We explored the area, with everyone choosing their preferred location to park their belongings and behinds. Some of us went for a walk, where we enjoyed a view of cliffs with sheltered beaches in little coves below. One spot was clearly a favourite for cliff-diving, with people lined up five or ten deep to take their turn at diving into the sea. Many cheered them on from below. While the height was scary to me, the divers clearly had local knowledge and the waters were deep and safe.

At a quieter spot, but just as steep, a Norwegian girl in our group mustered the courage to jump off the cliff into the deep water below. She was touched when I sent her pictures. It had been one of those moments where she'd allowed herself to get out of her comfort zone and overcome fear, and she was grateful that I'd managed to capture it on camera. I was too.

Gord is not much of a beach person in the traditional sense, meaning swimming and sunbathing, but he does like to walk along the beach and get his *passi* (steps) in. The thought takes me back to our most recent visit to Italy when we decided to walk the beaches for two hours a day. We'd head to a favourite spot and walk one hour out and one hour back. With the changing weather and light, it was often as if we were walking a different beach every day.

I have wonderful memories of exploring beaches in Sardinia during two separate visits to Italy's largest island. Sardinia is

known for its myriad of beaches, but it is impossible to generalise—
the almost 2,000 km of coastline is a continuum ranging from
sandy, gently-sloped beaches, to rugged cliffs. The beaches are as
diverse as the island's geology. You'll find some with soft white
sand, others covered in tiny quartz pebbles that look like grains
of rice, and there are wind-blown and water-eroded coastlines in
other areas with secluded coves only accessible by boat.

With Gord on my first visit, we explored the rocky
northwest coast, as well as some sandy beaches along the east
coast. While neither of us are lie-around-on-the-beach and
play-games-in-the-sand kind of people, the diversity and natural
beauty of the white sand beaches and crystal clear, iridescent
waters, and in some cases massive headlands and strange rock
formations, were more than enough to captivate me.

One of the loveliest beaches in northwest Sardinia is La
Pelosa, in Stintino, along a narrow strip of land that dwindles
into the sea near Asinara Island and its national park of the same
name. La Pelosa is extremely popular, owing to its long stretch
of fine white sand and shallow, turquoise waters. We chose
Spiaggia della Pelosetta (Little Pelosa), just north of the main
beach. We were hoping to avoid some of the crowds (though not
likely in August), and as I recall, because it was the only place
that we could find parking.

The entire area is gorgeous, so it's impossible to go wrong,
but overuse is an issue. We thought we were being taken in by
someone telling us that the mats he was trying to sell us were
required on the beach, but others confirmed they are mandatory—
to limit the amount of sand being lost from the beach we were
told. It is also an offence to intentionally remove sand or walk on
the dunes; and restrictions have been put in place to manage the
number of beachgoers in summer. These include an entrance fee,
described as a 'contribution to beach management'. A small price
to pay for this spectacular slice of nature.

The Riviera del Corallo (Coral Riviera), northwest of the seafront city of Alghero, is named after the vibrant red coral the area is famous for. Harvested from depths of 150 to 300 metres (unlike reef coral which is found in much shallower water), this precious coral has been used to make jewellery and ornaments since Roman times. You'll find it for sale in the many jewellery stores of Alghero but be mindful. Sardinian coral is prized for its natural rich hues and intense crimson colour, and authentic pieces will be priced accordingly. Unless you're prepared to crack open your wallet, you can expect to be paying for fake pieces. And prices of genuine red coral are only increasing as the quality and supply is compromised by over-fishing, which reduces regrowth potential, and by climate change, which creates issues such as acidification and detrimental changes in ocean temperatures.

Coral aside, along this piece of paradise you will find many beach options. Mugoni Beach is a narrow but long stretch of fine sand in the bay to the west of Alghero. With its soft sand and shallow waters, this beach is popular with families. What I enjoyed was the view across to Capo Caccia (literally 'hunting cape'—it was once a hunting reserve), a striking feature where the promontory drops almost 200 m into the sea.

The cliffs of Capo Caccia.

The limestone headland is home to many caves, some with spectacular developments of stalagmites and stalactites (elongated formations of minerals deposited over time from slowly dripping water). Neptune's Cave is the most famous. The grotto's entrance, which is just above sea level, can be reached by boat or by a winding stone stairway carved out of the side of the cliff. Although the 654 steps can be a deterrent for some, those who make the trek down, and back up of course, are rewarded with an exceptional display of these natural structures.

An amusing memory from our visit to Capo Caccia involved the Capo Caccia Hotel. It was apparently a four-star hotel in its time, with an impressive location overlooking the Gulf of Alghero, but the crumbling parking lot and dangling stars hanging off its sign suggested those days were long gone.

The Costa di Tentizzos shoreline between Alghero and the city of Bosa to the south, was another location I thoroughly enjoyed. I'd noticed a magazine article about the medieval town, highlighted as one of *i borghi più belli d'Italia* (the most beautiful villages of Italy), and felt compelled to visit. Like Alghero, Bosa has ancient origins, the area having been inhabited since prehistoric times. Today it is characterised by narrow pedestrian-only alleys and arcades, pastel-coloured houses, and elegant wrought-iron balconies. I loved the colourful reflections of the houses in the lazy Temo River that runs through town and found myself snapping more pictures than I knew what to do with. The red-arched *Ponte Vecchio* from the 1800s that crosses the Temo into the old town intensified the allure. The twelfth-century Malaspina Castle that dominates from above, provided villagers with much-needed protection in medieval times.

Along the nearby Costa di Tentizzos, I was struck by the white cliffs and their bizarre-looking shapes, constantly being resculpted by water and wind. They resembled a moonscape in some ways, yet it was dramatic and intriguing at the same time.

Perhaps the most interesting rocks I encountered were those with something called 'honeycomb weathering'. While many possible explanations have been proposed, there is agreement that the pattern is a result of a complex interplay between physical and chemical weathering processes. These processes typically occur in coarse-grained sedimentary or granite rock (rather than soluble rock such as limestone) and tend to be more common in salt-rich environments. Bingo to all three along the northwest coast of Sardinia where I found some exceptional examples of this honeycomb structure.

On a return trip to Sardinia, I was delighted to spend more time exploring the area with Rosanna. One day, after a hike along the rocky coast south of Porto Ferro, we returned to the car and continued to a crescent-shaped beach called Porticciolo (Little Port). I'd been hoping to end the day in a peaceful spot watching the sunset, and Rosanna delivered. The sandy beach circles a small cove overlooked by a medieval Spanish tower. We waded in for a dip, relaxing in the sun afterwards. I recall a feeling of absolute contentment as we watched a blazing orange ball sink below the horizon. As is often the case, the colours of the sky turned even more brilliant after the sun had set, lighting up with bright pinks and oranges and reds. I lingered to take it all in.

And while I didn't swim at every beautiful beach I visited, I did make a point of poking my toes into the water of as many as possible—such as in Santa Maria di Leuca at the most southerly tip of Apulia; near the quaint seaside town of Vieste on the Gargano promontory in Apulia; in the mountain stream running through the old spa town of Merano in South Tyrol; in the ancient coastal town of Cefalù and beside Isola Bella at the base of the resort town of Taormina, both in Sicily; and in an almost dried-up lake in the mountains above Courmayeur in Aosta Valley. These bring back fond memories of wonderful days well spent.

CHAPTER 13

Un Altro Bicchiere di Vino per Favore – Another Glass of Wine Please

Wine is the most civilized thing in the world.
—Ernest Hemingway

As well as being a passion of many Italians, wine is also an important aspect of their culture. Some say 'wine is culture' for Italians. With a climate that is perfectly suited to winemaking, Italy is one of the most prolific and diverse winemaking countries worldwide. Both the Romans and the Etruscans before them demonstrated a passion for winemaking, and wine has been at the centre of the Italian dining table ever since. My wine stories are more likely to make you laugh than anything, but hopefully you will do so with a full glass in hand.

Let me start with a sailing trip we took with friends. While exploring the port town on the small Tuscan island of Capraia, we came across a pattern of shallow wells carved out of rock just below the castle. I guessed it was a water filtration system. It turned out to be a series of centuries-old vats used for wine making, in use as recently as the eighteenth century. I marvelled at the creativity as well as how far winemaking has come. Where there's a will there's a way.

Returning to the twenty-first century, I have a vivid memory of sampling the homemade wine of Zio Paulo on our first visit to Fondi. Many consider the dining table bare without wine, and this lunch was no exception. I love dearly departed Paulo but thank goodness the glasses were small. Even so, I struggled. Let's just say it was 'fresh'. Luckily, we had brought a bottle with us and managed to make a little switch. That said, Paulo enjoyed his wine and that's what mattered.

I know even less about white wine than red, so perhaps I can be forgiven for this next story. Est! Est!! Est!!! is a wine region of Italy centred around the town of Montefiascone on Lake Bolsena. It is known for its white Trebbiano in particular. The story behind the unusual name of the wine region dates to a tale from the twelfth century, when a bishop was said to have been on his way to see the Pope. With a penchant for good wine, the bishop sent his scout ahead to test the local wines. When the scout tasted wine that he felt would impress the bishop, he would write 'Est' on the door (Latin for 'it is'). Finding the wine of Montefiascone to be so impressive, he wrote Est! Est!! Est!!!, the equivalent of three stars.

While at a nearby B&B with friends, two of whom were extremely passionate about their vino, our host suggested we visit Montefiascone. Look for 'Est! Est!! Est!!!' he said. We were unfamiliar with the name but were happy to give it a try. Driving from the 'dying city' of Civita di Bagnoregio, south to Montefiascone, we were greeted by an enormous Est! Est!! Est!!! sign. 'This has to be it!' we said to ourselves. We did some sampling and then bought a few bottles to take with us. Placing them on the dinner table that evening, our host was clearly surprised. 'Did you not find Montefiascone?' he inquired in Italian. *Sì*. 'Is there a problem?' As we learned, Est! Est!! Est!!! is known for white wine, not the reds we had purchased. Now he tells us!

The designation 'dying city' references the progressive erosion of rock beneath the ancient hill town of Civita, a combination of clay from an ancient seabed topped by volcanic *tufo* (tuff rock). Both are soft rocks and susceptible to erosion that has been exacerbated by deforestation in the surrounding valley. At one point connected by land to Bagnoregio, the old city of Civita now appears as if perched atop a weather-beaten island in the middle of an enormous canyon of badlands. The only access is via a long footbridge. It is distinctive to say the least, and the history of this little town is as captivating as the landscape. The main entrance, Porto Santa Maria, is an enormous stone passageway constructed by the Etruscans over 2,500 years ago. Walking through it is like a trip back in time.

Inside we found a charming and peaceful town adorned by pots of flowers wherever you looked. Most of the activity takes place around the small central piazza enclosed by the church (of course), as well as a few small but lively cafes and restaurants offering local fare. We sat with at one of the cafes flanking the main square and were happy to absorb the ambience.

I was also reminded of an elderly lady I met here quite a few years earlier. While walking along a passageway that extended out from the main piazza, a woman, who looked to be at least in her eighties, waved us over. She wanted us to follow her behind the houses to see *un gardino,* a garden. We were happy

The dying city of Civita di Bagnoregio.

to oblige, although honestly, the view and the garden were nothing we had not already seen. She then put her hand out for a 'donation'. I wasn't even certain the garden was hers, but how could we refuse? She was adorable and it was money well spent.

I also toured Montalcino, famous for its Brunello reds, and Montepulciano, known for its classic Vino Nobile—both medieval hill towns with expansive views of the valleys below. On two separate occasions I had fun in Montepulciano with a man who sold his Vino Nobile with unbridled enthusiasm and offered *baci* on the side (kisses, on the cheek) for good measure. That said, my favourite experience was at Villa Nottola, a family-run winery just outside Montepulciano. We were on our way into town, but my friends were ready to jump out as soon as the first opportunity arose. Fortuitous or not, it proved to be a great choice. One of the daughters and the fiancé of a son were our guides and could not have been more amicable. Language was a barrier, but we had fun with the tastings, and I worked my Italian to pick up what I could about the family and history of their winery.

Just a note. Cantine Aperte is an initiative that was started in 1993 to promote wine tourism in Italy. It involves wineries across the country, including over one hundred in Tuscany alone. In certain months of the year cellars are opened to the public for free guided tours and tastings. There are also various related activities and programs depending on the region. We happened to be in Tuscany at the end of May one year when the doors of wineries across the region were open. No appointment required. English was scant, but we managed to learn a thing or two and taste some memorable vino.

While staying at B&B Gatta Morena by myself one year, I was treated to a weekend on their charter sailboat. We sailed from a marina in Punta Ala (Tuscany) across to Elba Island, where our captain, Pino, found a quiet bay to anchor. After a welcome swim, several of us tendered to shore in a small dingy. There was no debate about which route to hike, as the only option was a dirt road heading up. The views became more dramatic as we climbed, the hillsides laced with vineyards; rows and rows of grape vines dropping away to the sea. As we continued our hike, we bumped into an elderly gentleman out for a walk of his own. He lived in a nearby villa on his family's estate, prestigious Tenuta della Ripalta. Following a short conversation, we were invited back to the hotel and winery for a degustazione, as his guests no less.

He led us down to the tasting bar where we were introduced to a hostess who served us the various estate wines. Looking online after the fact, I learned that this was a significant winery on Elba, producing DOC (Denomination of Origin Controlled) wines characteristic of the island, including a DOCG wine that has been made for centuries. DOC certifies where the wine is from, that it was made using a controlled production method, and that it meets a government standard for quality. A DOCG label, such as those noted below, additionally guarantees the wine to be of the highest quality in Italy. Much of the wine production on Elba Island has been displaced because of tourism, although I was pleased to read that an association is working to ensure the protection of Elba DOC wines.

Valpolicella is another famous Tuscan wine region, where wine making has existed at least since the time of the ancient Greeks. The region is flanked by Lake Garda to the west and Verona, of Romeo and Juliet fame, to the southeast, and is second only to Italy's Chianti wine region in total production.

The Serego Alighieri Estate is in the heart of the Valpolicella Classico wine district. After being owned by descendants of the famous poet Dante Alighieri for twenty-one generations, the family found itself with only a female heir. The solution? She was married into the powerful Serego family, after which their descendants used the combined surname. Over time, this historic estate grew to become one of the most esteemed wine producers in the region, with wine-making traditions dating back more than 650 years. The estate came under the umbrella of the Masi Group in 1973 who, together with Count Serego Alighieri, work to produce premium wines. One example is Amarone, a rich DOCG red wine. I was interested in seeing how the grapes were partially dried on straw mats prior to fermentation. The labour-intensive and time-consuming process of course adds to the cost.

I first visited the estate with two Canadian friends, Mario and Joan, in part thanks to Mario's 'Cousin Tony', who is a representative for Masi. With Cousin Tony's blessing, the three of us were treated to a stay in this elegant villa. I loved the place so much that I found a way to return with my husband a few years later. On this visit we were remarkably fortunate to run into the president of Masi Agricola Wine, Mr. Sandro Boscaini. He had recently written a book and offered to sign it for us. He was busy with guests when we were leaving, but as promised a signed copy arrived after we got home. Mr. Boscaini was a friendly man and clearly passionate about the wine his family had produced for generations.

La Casaccia, Piedmont

Until last year I would have said that, without a doubt, my favourite Italian wine experience was from our stay at Il Colle. I talked about Giovanni from Il Colle earlier. His passion for life—and for his Chianti Classico—was contagious. Then I met another Giovanni, this one at Agriturismo La Casaccia in the Monferrato wine district. This Giovanni, too, loves his wine like he loves his family.

Giovanni loading grapes in the vineyard
at Agriturismo La Casaccia.

For some background, I was at La Casaccia as a volunteer, working in exchange for room and board. I had been looking for a way to extend my stays in Italy without breaking the bank, to practise my Italian and, as much as possible, to live like a local. After joining the association for Worldwide Workers on Organic Farms (WWOOF), I had access to a host of options, doing anything from making wine or cheese or olive oil or honey to helping raise goats and chickens. Some places were working to bring ancient olive groves or vineyards back into production, others were making essential oils from their herb gardens. Some had full services, and others asked you to live in a tent and use a compostable outhouse. *No, grazie!* I knew with utmost certainty that the latter was not my cup of vino.

I chose La Casaccia for several reasons—in addition to the fact that it had indoor plumbing. A major draw was its location; it was in Piedmont, a region I was interested in spending more time exploring. I was in Piedmont for two weeks during the

World Masters Games, but my visit had been limited to the city of Turin. The fact that La Casaccia was an agriturismo as well as a winery was also appealing. It meant there would be diversity in terms of the type of work I might be asked to help with and, therefore, in what I could learn. With their vegetarian lifestyle and concern for the environment, I was convinced I would enjoy La Casaccia, and I was bang on. I don't think I could have chosen a better place to fit my interests.

To get to La Casaccia from where I was in Sardinia, I flew to Milan and rented a car for the one-hour drive to Casale Monferrato. Margherita, the daughter, was to pick me up at the rental agency's office where I was leaving the vehicle. I would have been happy to take the bus from Milan, but the connections were messy due to my arrival time. I was in no hurry driving, as Margherita had messaged that she would be late. The grapes were ready for picking and it was all hands on deck.

I made myself comfortable in the waiting room when I got to Casale, chatting with the friendly attendant between customers, sipping on a coffee he offered, and learning about the best ski resorts in the area. It was Giovanni, Margherita's father, who eventually arrived in his farm truck, apologising that he had come straight from the fields. I loved him from the start, a small man with a big smile, and we chatted in Italian during the twenty-minute drive back to Celle Monte. He spoke clearly, which was extremely helpful. And with the benefit of a week in Sardinia to get my r's rolling and my ear attuned to the language, my Italian was flowing—not always the case, but it didn't let me down on this occasion.

Cella Monte is a tiny place but driving into the family's courtyard convinced me that I was right where I was meant to be. It was hard to believe this was going to be my home for three glorious weeks. The villa and *cantina* (cellar) had some distinctive features. Built in the 1800s by their noble ancestors, it was an elegant home surrounding a lovely courtyard. A central grassy area, where two lawn chairs lay in waiting, was surrounded by pretty trees and flowers, and planters with all the herbs an Italian cook would need. Sitting under a large canopy was an elegant dining table, made from long, beautifully finished pieces of wood—two sides of a large tree folded open to expose the grain. I shared many enjoyable meals at that table.

The outdoor dining table at La Casaccia.

Inside, the villa felt enormous, with an enclosed kitchen and dining table at the heart of the home. My bedroom was in a rarely used wing that housed four stately rooms extended along a wide hallway that ended in a massive bathroom, clawfoot tub and all. Two of the four bedrooms were reserved for *ospiti*, B&B guests, but there were few during my stay (generally the case during the busy harvest season). Across the hall was Antonia's room, the young gal who had arrived from Copenhagen a week after me. I thought I would prefer to be on my own but soon realised how delightful it was to have her company.

The two of us worked together at times, whether helping host B&B guests, assisting with wine tours and tastings, or working in the gardens and vineyards. Or one of us might be asked to assist in the kitchen and the other in the cantina. One day Antonia and I wiped down every leaf and branch of the several lemon trees in the yard. Apparently, there is a little bug that likes to eat the leaves but does not like alcohol, so that was our eco-friendly chore for a day.

After finishing an assigned task, I would look for something else to do—hanging laundry or dead-heading flowers, for example. The family had welcomed me into their home, and I was keen to be of assistance where I could. Watering the plants was a time-consuming task, given the size of the yard and the effort it took to move the long, heavy hose. I laugh thinking about my first attempt. After being at it for a while, Margherita yelled from the cantina below. 'Stop!' I was overwatering and the excess was draining down into the cellar. Water was dripping everywhere. 'Maybe a little less next time!' she suggested.

Monferrato forms a rough triangle between the cities of Turin, Milan, and Genoa. The climate is influenced by the cooling Alps to the north and the balmy Mediterranean to the south. Together they cause a wide variation in day and night temperatures that creates a recipe for good wine. From my window I had a sweeping view of the rolling hills to the northeast. I would stand on the stairwell balcony many mornings, just gazing at the beauty. I can't count how many pictures I took of the hilltops rising above the mist that hung in the valley floors, with rays of the rising sun starting to bounce off the vineyards above the fog. I learned that the fog helps make this area perfect for cultivating its famous

Barbera grapes. The vineyards above the foggy layer receive more warmth and sunshine, just what the grapes crave.

Most wine enthusiasts associate Piedmont with the full-bodied reds of Barolo, but it has much more to offer, including over 42 DOC and 17 DOCG certified wines. La Casaccia produces a Barbera del Monferrato as well as several other wines typical of this wine zone. Although Barbera d'Asti and d'Alba are the better-known ones, all three boast a DOC designation.

Before arriving at La Casaccia, I had no idea what an 'infernot' was. Reading the English translation on the winery's internet site, I assumed it was an error, but it was my error. The word originates from French for 'tight space' and refers to historic underground rooms for storing bottled wine. The rooms were hand-carved into the *pietra da cantoni*, as it's called, a type of sandstone formed beneath the sea that covered this area 20 million years ago. This unique construction has been found only in a specific portion of Monferrato, right in the middle of where I happened to be staying. *Che fortuna!* How lucky!

When farmers started to bottle their wine in the 1700s, many began to dig these cave-like spaces at the base of their cellars. The intention was to create perfect conditions for storing the bottles by keeping the temperature and humidity as stable as possible. The marks of the picks used to dig out the rooms are still evident. In many cases the infernot have built-in shelving carved out of the rock, and even tables carved out of the floor. Those who tour these facilities may also see some of the fossils and shells that are remnants from the ancient seabed. There currently are almost one hundred surveyed infernot in Monferrato, and I was staying at a historic villa that had its very own. If that were not enough to satisfy my interest, I only had to walk up the street to the Ecomuseo della Pietra da Cantoni, a small museum in Cella Monte where I could learn more about the history of the infernot.

The territories of Langhe, Monferrato, and Roero were collectively the first wine district in the world recognised by UNESCO. The designation relates to the area's history (wine has been made here since ancient Roman times) and the extraordinary landscape shaped by humans in the form of viticulture (grape growing) and viniculture (wine making). Part of the appeal in visiting the area is that the UNESCO site is not found in only one landmarked location. Rather, it is spread out across the three territories and includes specific vineyard areas, underground 'cathedrals' (big cellars where sparkling wines age), and the infernot of Monferrato.

While volunteering at La Casaccia I was exposed to many aspects of the wine-making process, from picking and crushing the grapes to filtration and fermentation. And when I say exposed, I mean hands-on involved. We picked grapes and hauled them from the fields, washed and dried every carton used to transport them, cleaned out the grape press machine, cleaned and stacked the filters, scrubbed down the cantina to keep the inevitable mould at bay, washed and rewashed the many hoses used to transport the must from the pressing machine through the filters and into the storage tanks. The only part I missed was bottling, and I loved it all. Well, maybe not the two days in the damp cellars scrubbing down everything, but we appreciated that Margherita was with us. We all worked side by side, stopping for lunch together, and continued until the job was done.

As a relatively small, family-run operation, there were tricks and techniques to everything: ways to hang the hoses so that water did not pool in them and cause mould, the right and wrong way to put the filters together, how to stack the crates so they dried in the sun. In the field we picked in pairs. Any questions and I had someone to ask. We all picked on the same side of the vines for safety. Slightly shrivelled grapes were okay, but ones that looked more like raisins had to go. They would impact the acidity of the wine. Knock off the bad grapes with the pliers and keep the rest of the bunch.

I think my favourite activity was helping with the tastings. Margherita would take couples or small groups on a tour of the winery, followed by a tasting in the garden. One group of Dutch gals was hysterical. The price of tours varied depending on the number of wines sampled. The group initially asked to sample three bottles, which included an antipasto and *grissini* (crunchy breadsticks) with each. After laughing their way through these bottles, the gals decided they needed to go for the five-pack. They were having such a good time that we had trouble getting them to leave. Fortunately, they were staying nearby and had walked over. I also remember these ladies because, when they learned I was Canadian, one asked if I knew where Fort Saskatchewan was. She had just visited a friend there. As big as Canada is, I did. I live about thirty minutes away. What a crazy small world.

A highlight of sorts for me was conducting a wine tour *da sola* (by myself). I was excited and petrified at the same time. I'm not quite sure how I managed, to be honest, since I knew next to nothing about wine just a couple of weeks earlier, and the large group spoke next to no English. The family had left for the weekend to take care of business elsewhere. Elena mentioned that a 'friend of a friend' may be coming by to pick up some wine. No problem. Margherita also gave me a run-down on where the various bottles of wine they sold were stored, and the price for each. She didn't want to turn away business if a customer happened to stop by. It all sounded harmless. But things did not unfold quite as anticipated.

A group of seven or eight Italians arrived in late afternoon, asking for their wine. Antonia and I looked everywhere, even messaging Margherita, to no avail. One of the men called his friend (who I assume was the friend Elena had mentioned). Speaking in Italian, he explained the situation, and that there was a woman here *che non sa nulla*—who doesn't know anything! We all laughed. They knew I understood. And he was correct. I had no idea where his wine was. In my defence, Elena's understanding was that someone might come by to purchase wine, but none had been pre-ordered or set aside.

The excitement didn't stop there. The group was interested in a tour of the winery. More specifically, they wanted to see La Casaccia's historic infernot. The adventure continued.

I'd been on several tours with Margherita and picked up some information from those. Coincidentally, I had also just visited the local infernot museum that morning, which infused me with confidence. When I struggled to find the Italian word I was looking for, someone was able to fill in the blank. I showed them the 2,400 bottles of Spumante that Antonia and I had cleaned and marked, one by one, in preparation for riddling (the tilted bottles are rotated a quarter turn every day for a set period as part of the production process). I pointed out the various vats where the wines were fermenting, and the bottling machine. I explained how the cantina was carved by hand, and the blocks then used to construct the villa above. And lastly, I guided them down to the infernot.

At the end of my tour, I thanked them for coming and said I'd be happy to answer any questions, though I had already shared everything I knew. To my relief they laughed. For someone who is by no means fluent, I was proud of myself. They even bought some wine, which I knew Elena would be happy about.

I can't leave La Casaccia without sharing one more hysterical story. One evening before dinner, Giovanni and Elena started a yeast mixture for fermenting the grapes that we had just picked, crushed, and filtered.

Distracted by dinner conversation, no one was paying attention until I looked up to see a huge mess bubbling over the pot on the stove. The mixture seemed to have a mind of its own, oozing everywhere. There was too much laughter to figure out exactly what had happened, but somehow the yeast had been left for too long, or perhaps had too much sugar. Either way, it had gotten way out of control and created quite a mess. It was nice to see Elena and Giovanni laughing over the whole fiasco.

Oh, there is one more thing. Not about wine, but about what Giovanni did in his 'free' time. He had a pet project with others in the area, using pigs to clear the bush in an area of overgrown vineyards. The idea was to get the land back into production, and in the process raise pigs that could eventually garner a coveted DOP designation, like Prosciutto di Parma, or the famous Iperico ham of Spain. Giovanni would wake early to check on his pigs and was often also gone in the evening. He'd bring them treats from the garden or compost—rotting chestnuts were a favourite. We could smell exactly where he'd been. Even though it was often late, Elena would insist he shower before dinner, which we were certainly on board with.

Wine is such an integral part of the Italian lifestyle and my hands-on experience at La Casaccia was an ideal way to learn more about this aspect of Italian culture. Seeing and feeling the passion they lived their lives with is what drew me to both Giovanni's. And it is through the layers of these experiences that Italy continued to reveal itself to me.

CHAPTER 14

Trekking e Ciclismo – Hiking and Biking

The world reveals itself to those who travel on foot.
—Werner Herzog

As an avid hiker and biker, I looked for opportunities to pursue both interests in Italy. Whether on foot or bicycle, both were great ways to get exercise while seeing the sights in a more up close and personal way. Unfortunately, my adventures did not always work out quite as planned. That said, they connected me with locals and there were some valuable lessons learned along the way.

During an early-on visit to Fondi, I asked about hiking up Monte Passignano (Monte Petrulo to locals), the hill we could see from our balcony. Despite having lived there during his childhood, Joe had never climbed it. I believe his response was something to the effect that Italians are not hikers. 'Well,' I said, 'I'm going to climb it.' Seeing my determination, he agreed to join us, but suggested we first take a reconnaissance trip to the back of the hill to scout out our options. After a discussion with locals, we had our game plan, and the next day we returned for the ascent.

At the insistence of Joe's mother, I was dressed in knee-high socks and long shorts, for fear I might get bitten by a snake. How she determined this was a real possibility I'm not sure, but I did as I was told. I pulled together a geeky-looking outfit, borrowing long, soccer socks as I recall, and away we went. The climb took under an hour, but the elevation was enough to provide a sweeping view over Fondi and even out to *il mare*—the Tyrrhenian Sea. I remember a little emotion from Joe as he sat gazing over the valley. It was a new perspective on his hometown.

I have an intrinsic dislike for 'out and back' hikes. My motto is to just keep going, usually finding a way to make a loop rather than having to retrace my steps. As you might imagine, this strategy did not always serve me well and added unintended adventure to several excursions. When on my own in Italy, I would often pull on my runners and go exploring. With no fixed agenda, I was happy to follow any road or path that looked interesting. On more occasions than I care to admit, I ended up having to climb fences, scramble through bushes, or snake my way through rocky terraces lined with olive trees. Once, after a long, hot hike, I emerged from the hilly olive groves into someone's yard—and, of course, the owners were right there. *Buon giorno*, I offered. *È questa la strada per Fondi?* Is this the path to Fondi? It was not a hiking path by any stretch, but they appeared unfazed by my abrupt appearance. Other than a few scratches, my misadventures happily did not land me in any real trouble, for the most part.

While I'm accustomed to getting myself into tricky situations, I prefer not to get friends lost, as was the unfortunate case on a walk around Bolsena. Among other things, the city is known for a miracle that is said to have occurred in the Basilica of Santa Cristina in 1263, when a priest reported bleeding from the communion bread he had consecrated. The appearance of blood was considered a miracle, as it seemed to affirm the Catholic doctrine which states that the consecrated bread and wine become the body and blood of Christ. Miracle or not, it is a pretty place to visit.

After wandering through the attractive streets and then down to the lake shore, I fatefully chose a different route back. Walking through olive groves and past chicken coops, it was clear I was leading my friends very much astray. Eventually we made our way to the Rocca Monaldeschi (the castle above town), which proved to be a useful landmark in this instance, and from there found our way to the car. It was a longer walk than any of us had planned, the faces of my friends glowing red from the heat, but it was nothing a stiff aperitivo could not take care of.

I first learned about the Via Francigena, which translates to 'the road that comes from France', when I spotted signposts on a walk around Fondi. With a little investigating I learned that the signs point the way to an ancient pilgrim route running from Canterbury to France, and then through Switzerland to Italy. The Via was the main route from northern Europe to Rome in the Middle Ages, with a range of options for crossing the Alps and Apennine Mountains. From Rome, the path follows ancient roads such as Via Appia (the Appian Way) and eventually makes its way to Bari, Brindisi, and Otranto, the main ports for travel to Jerusalem.

Since medieval times, pilgrims have followed this path. The food and shelter required by these early travellers fuelled the growth of communities around churches and taverns along the way as pilgrims brought wealth and fostered development. Though less popular today than the Camino Santiago in Spain, Via Francigena is a classic pilgrim's walk that traverses several Italian regions. I have followed the social media posts of various hikers on their journey and it is something I hope to undertake myself one day.

During a tour of the southern region of Campania with my husband and brother, we decided to hike the popular Mount Vesuvius trail. We were impressed to find a man handing out free walking sticks, but we should have known there were strings attached. On our way down he was asking for 'donations'. The sticks had served us well, however, and we were happy to contribute. The volcano's rim features a lunar-like landscape, complete with steam venting from the crater. While it has been quiet since 1944, the volcano's massive eruption in 79 AD buried the Roman cities of Pompeii and Herculaneum under mounds of mud and volcanic material, leaving the ancient cities frozen in time. They were rediscovered in the eighteenth century and restoration work continues.

In the Valpolicella wine area of Veneto, we took a gondola ride up to the ridge of Monte Baldo, a mountain range in the Italian Alps that dominates the east side of Lake Garda. It is a popular skiing area in winter and equally popular for hiking and biking in summer. After a dazzling hike along the ridge, followed by a picnic lunch with breathtaking views overlooking the northern end of the lake, we made our way back to the gondola. On our way down, one of us had the bright idea to get off at the mid-way station and hike the remainder of the way. Although this might not have been a bad idea in theory, the short-cut we opted to take certainly was. It was extremely steep, with loose stones for a good portion of the route. Neither of us had proper footwear, never mind our combination of bad knees and ankles. The trail was less than 500 m according to the sign that lured us in, but with an almost 600 m elevation drop it seemed considerably longer as we tentatively picked our way down. With the temperature soaring, I felt beat up by the time we worked our way to the bottom. To sum things up, I absolutely earned my gelato that day.

Rosanna is more concerned with safety than speed when driving, but on one occasion her speed-demon friend Carlos was at the wheel, insisting that his driving was *più efficiente*, more efficient. I had to laugh; that was the excuse I used for driving too fast, contending it is a waste of time to drive slowly. Unlike Carlos, I have since rethought that one.

Knowing it would be busy at the beach, we wanted to get there in good time, but for some reason we still stopped for coffee. I've decided this is just what Italians do. And when we did arrive at Costa Paradiso, along Sardinia's northern coast, there was no parking to be found, not surprisingly, since it was late August and prime beach time. In the end we drove back along the coast to an alternative access point at Spiaggia del Tinnari. It meant a half-hour hike to the beach, but the view of the gleaming water below had us hurrying to get down.

After a refreshing swim, which included checking out the intriguing Roccia Spaccata (Split Rock) in the middle of the little bay, and a light lunch, Rosanna and I decided to hike back to Costa Paradiso, following a rugged trail that hugged the shoreline. Carlos would pick us up. It was a highlight of the day for me—an energetic hike, amazing views at every turn, and great company to chat with along the way (other than when we fell silent to enjoy our surroundings). I could not get over how stunning it all was, the characteristic red rocks, distinctively shaped by the elements, plunging into the blue-green waters along our route. Unable to resist, we stopped at least two more times for a dip, including at a spot known for its natural swimming pools. We arrived at Costa Paradiso later than planned, but our chauffeur was unconcerned. Clearly no one was in any hurry to get home, as we again stopped along the way, this time for aperitivo. Our drinks came with some snacks, and we also indulged in a selection of dolce from the bakery next door.

And if that was not enough for one day, Carlos had caught fish the day before and wanted to grill them for our dinner, along with fresh mussels. To prepare the *pesci* he just smothered them with salt—to keep the fish moist, he said in Italian. While the ladies visited in the kitchen, he stoked the fire until the embers were red hot. Rosanna had brought fresh figs from her garden, which she cut open (the skin is so soft you can eat it too) and filled with bresaola (thinly sliced, cured and aged beef), soft burrata cheese, and bright red pomegranate seeds. With large fig leaves decorating the plate, the platter looked like a piece of art. It was a wonderful evening for reasons beyond the food. Although Carlos and his wife didn't know me, as a friend of Rosanna's I was welcomed with open arms. It was a day I won't forget.

Carlos had the fire going and fish ready.

I'm also reminded of a hike into the Foresta di Montes park area in central Sardinia. We met Rosanna's friend here, a park ranger who escorted us to the ancient trailhead for Monte Novo San Giovanni. On our way, he stopped so we could fill our water bottles from the fountain at the *sorgente* (source) of the Cedrino River, a main river of Sardinia that flows into the Gulf of Orosei on the island's east coast. The hike itself took maybe an hour, through a bit of forest and then rock outcrops to the summit. In addition to the spectacular views from the top, over the Gennargentu Massif (which includes the highest peaks on the island), there was a small hut used as a fire lookout, complete with a ranger asleep along a sun-soaked bench.

Another ranger came out of the hut and struck up a conversation with Rosanna, eventually inviting us in for an espresso. Gord declined, and was instantly offered some grappa instead, which was much more to his liking. The sleeping worker managed to wake himself—just in time for coffee break. It was an unexpected but most enjoyable experience, initiated simply by engaging in conversation.

Back at the bottom, we met up with Rosanna's friend again and followed him to another rudimentary ranger's station for lunch. His packed lunch consisted of hard pecorino cheese and *pane carasau*, traditional Sarda flatbread also known as 'music sheets' because it is so thin. Balls of dough are kneaded and then rolled into thin flat rounds that are baked in hot stone ovens until the dough swells up like a ball, with an air pocket inside. The bread is removed, the thin top and bottom layers carefully separated, and then each is placed back in the oven to finish baking. An ancient bread that dates back thousands of years, its light and crispy texture helps it last longer without going stale; perfect for the shepherds who used to spend extended periods away from home. It is still popular and easily found in grocery stores or bakeries. I tried a piece but didn't think much of it. Luckily, Rosanna had packed a lunch for us.

The grappa story brings to mind a similar experience in Aosta Valley, the small region snuggled up in the northwest corner of the country below France and Switzerland. We were on a hike suggested by the owner of our B&B when we came across a herd of cows being rounded up by a weathered herdsman. We paused to say hello, and somehow managed to get ourselves invited into his mountain hut for a glass of homemade grappa. I tried to decline, fearing I might be tasting it for the rest of our hike, but Armand insisted. I thought he said it was made with honey (*miele*), but it could have been apples (*mele*) now that I think about it. Either way, I agreed to try it and was pleasantly surprised. It was the best grappa I have tasted, homemade or otherwise; strong, but sweet and smooth at the same time.

Gord and Armand enjoying some grappa.

While sipping our grappa, Armand showed us a calendar featuring cows with prize ribbons. I later learned that the Battle of the Queens is an annual contest in which cows compete for the title of Queen of Horns. In pairs, they push each other around until one of them falls over, and eventually a queen is crowned. I believe one of Armand's cows had recently been awarded the prestigious crown. Regardless, he clearly was enthusiastic about his herd.

Armand was also a truly kind man. His goats had been grazing on the grassy roof of his hut, which was built into the side of the hill, but they'd moved on by the time we came out. When Armand realised that I was hoping for a picture, he ran inside to get a piece of bread and then used it to coax the goats back onto the roof. He got a few to cooperate while I took pictures, some of which I sent him later. I hope to see one hanging beside the calendars of Armand's famous cows the next time I make that trek.

With Armand and his goats in the glorious Alps.

The hike got even more interesting after we left Armand. The owner of Rifugio Mont Fallère, where we were heading, was also a wood carver, and all along the upper portion of the route were dozens of carvings. At the top we were rewarded with a view across the valley to Gran Paradiso, the highest peak in the national park of the same name, and the tallest mountain solely in Italy. The place was buzzing with hikers and bikers, some eating and drinking, others relaxing in the sunshine. I treated myself to a regional favourite, polenta with cheese; it certainly provided a carb load for the hike down.

I learned a lesson about these mountain huts some time ago while hiking above Merano, referred to as the Gateway to the Dolomites. We had packed a lunch for our hike that ended at a rifugio about two hours later. After purchasing a beer inside, we found a sunny spot on the deck to relax and enjoy the views. Shortly after pulling out our sandwiches, the manager paid us a visit. He was polite but made it clear that it was not appropriate to be eating our packed lunch on his terrace. It is common to bring your lunch into a ski lodge in Canada, so we can hopefully be forgiven for not appreciating the difference here. Lesson learned.

The Dolomites continue the network of mountain refuges and extensive hiking trails across northern Italy. My sister and I had an opportunity to climb to Rifugio Locatelli at the base of the renowned Tre Cime di Lavaredo (Three Peaks of Lavaredo) in the Trentino-Alto Adige region. This was a challenging hike for us, with a stiff 2,450 m ascent. While appreciating the fabulous mountain views, we found hearty ethnic dishes, decadent desserts, and hot and cold beverages on offer for weary hikers. Then, all we had to do was get back down.

My sister and the Tre Cime di Lavaredo.

Although it requires some effort, the route between the five villages of Cinque Terre is a great way to see the wild coast and the ancient villages impossibly packed into the cliffs above the sea. Unfortunately, the trail is often crowded, not only with hikers but with flip-flopping tourists who decide to take a walk in the park. And in 2011, the area was hit by a violent storm with record-breaking rainfall that precipitated landslides. It was a devastating event with long-lasting consequences. Vernazza, one of the five villages, was the hardest hit, with rivers of sludge and debris flooding through it, causing massive destruction and costing lives. The paths linking the villages were also damaged in several areas and portions remain off limits (check with park authorities for updates).

In addition to its DOC white wine, and olives grown on the terraced slopes above the villages, the area is also known for its basil pesto and limoncello liqueur. Order a pasta with pesto sauce and you can't go wrong. I also remember being treated on one occasion to something called *farinata*, a savoury pancake-type snack made from a base of chickpea flour. The restaurant owner wanted us to try it along with his limoncello, and we certainly had no objections. My several experiences in this area made it easy to appreciate why the five villages were designated a World Heritage site by UNESCO in 1997 for 'the harmonious interaction between people and nature to produce a landscape of exceptional scenic quality'.

Equally as stunning is the hike south from Riomaggiore (the most southerly of the five towns) to Portovenere, a favourite location of writers and poets, such as Byron, Shelley, D. H. Lawrence, and others. After about 12 km, the trail descends (rather steeply I might add) into Portovenere, just above the Church of St. Peter. Easily spotted by its black-and-white striped facade, the pretty church sits precariously on a rocky promontory that overlooks the Gulf of La Spezia (also known as the Bay of Poets). Below the church, in the cliffs edging the Gulf, you will find remnants of Byron's Grotto, from where he is said to have swum across the bay to visit Shelley.

On a side note, it is funny how memory works. While hiking this trail we came across a deli in the village of Campiglia where they build your sandwich according to the amount and type of meat and cheese you want. The server started to slice the meat I had chosen and then asked *Basta?* I had never heard the word before but knew instantly what she meant. *Si, basta. Grazie!* Yes, enough. Thank you. My new word for the day.

Hiking tends to offer better views than biking, unless of course you go to Italy in search of the tallest summits to conquer like a couple of my super fit friends do. But biking provides the opportunity to cover more territory and still have a more intimate experience with the world around than is possible in a car. I could smell the cypress trees, hear the incessant crickets, stop and take photographs at will, and chat with locals as I checked my directions.

In Apulia, the heel of the Italian boot, which claims more coastline than any other mainland region, I could cycle to both the east (Adriatic) and west (Ionian) coasts of the peninsula from where I was staying. On afternoon breaks from my yoga training I would borrow one of the rather clumsy bicycles and start riding. It was not an ideal time of day to be biking, since it was the hottest part of already hot July days, but afternoons were our only free time, so I took what I could get.

One day I ended up in Gallipoli, a city of Greek origin that has a long and storied history thanks to its strategic position on the Ionian coast (and not to be confused with the Turkish city of Gallipoli that was the scene of a disastrous Allied campaign in World War I). The old town is on a tiny island attached to the mainland by a short bridge, with a thirteenth-century Byzantine castle and thick protective walls greeting visitors.

Inside the walls is a tangle of streets laden with shops and cafes. Ornate Baroque churches and palaces display the city's former prosperity. I found a quiet spot on a sandy beach, just below the wall that surrounds the old town, to slip into the water for a break from the relentless sun before beginning my return trip.

On another day I cycled to Otranto, a town with a similar history due to its location on the eastern side of the peninsula, facing Greece and the Balkans. My tour of the town's historic centre included the eleventh-century cathedral, famous for its Tree of Life mosaic floor and the 800 martyrs who defied the invading Turks in 1480. I followed up with a refreshing swim in the tranquil waters of the Adriatic Sea and a rest in the little park just outside the walls that mark the entrance to the old town. It was hard to get on my bike after that for the trip home.

In Fondi I borrowed bikes whenever possible. The roads are not designed for biking, evidenced by regular accidents with farm workers cycling to and from work on roads with non-existent shoulders. Still, I took every opportunity to explore the area and surrounding countryside, such as Terracina on the coast (a seaside resort town with a history going back to antiquity) and the quaint village of Lenola in the hills above Fondi. That was a challenging climb. On the upside, it took next to no time to get back down. I could see the attraction for Joe's dad cruising into work all those years ago. Joe's Aunt Gina joked that I knew the area better than she did even though she had lived there all her life. For me, the bike was freedom—a way to see more of the area and to broaden my experiences through unplanned encounters.

The two weeks I spent biking around Turin during the World Masters Games provided me with many more unplanned opportunities to explore and connect. In preparation for the opening ceremonies, teams were asked to congregate in Piazza Vittorio Veneto, just north of the Po River. The energy was palpable. From there we paraded up elegant Via Po, with soaring porticoes on both sides, to Piazza Castello. Spectators lined the route, waving excitedly and taking pictures of us, as we in turn waved and took pictures of them. In the Piazza, surrounded by some of the most elaborate architectural jewels the city has to offer, we stood for speeches and celebrations that kicked off the Games. So began my love affair with Turin.

I had an injury that unfortunately kept me from competing in my sport, but the upside was that I could spend time touring the city. Turin's hop-on, hop-off bike system was a huge bonus. Like many large cities, the 'yellow-bike system', as I called it, allowed me to pick up a bike close to where my sister and I were staying and then drop it off at my destination. Between the sporting events I took in, I could explore much more territory on a bike than would have been possible on foot.

Those bikes took me to places like Piazza San Carlo, affectionately referred to as Turin's 'drawing room'. Framed by a series of interconnected porticoes, a distinguishing heritage feature of the Piedmontese capital, the elegant arcades and surrounding palazzos made this an inviting place to linger. The Piazza is also home to some of Turin's most famous cafes, such as Caffè Torino and Caffè San Carlos, haunts of intellectual, cultural and political leaders since the nineteenth century. I must say it was a little intimidating ordering inside Caffè Torino, with its ornate Art Nouveau architecture and glamorous decor, but I managed!

Along the banks of the Po River, I explored the city's largest park, Parco del Valentino, which houses botanical gardens, a replica medieval village, and lavish Castello del Valentino. The castle is a UNESCO World Heritage site, one of numerous heritage-listed Residences of the Royal House of Savoy, recognized for their 'monumental architecture'. The twenty-one structures included in the designation were built by the Duchy in and around Turin from the late sixteenth century.

I rode the paths that edged the meandering Po River, and the smaller rivers that feed into it, and pretty much poked my nose into every corner of the city that caught my fancy. Turin had a different look and feel than other Italian cities I had visited to date, and I couldn't get enough of it.

Occasionally, if there were no bikes available, I would walk a short distance to the next stand to get my wheels; it never took long to find a bike at one location or another. And if my destination was outside the bike zone, I'd leave my bike at the closest stand and walk from there. I would have been happier playing soccer, but I loved every minute of it. And notwithstanding all that Turin had to offer, perhaps the biggest thrill was seeing my sister and some of her former volleyball teammates from the Canadian National Team win their age-category final to clinch the gold medal. That was special.

Biking along the Po River in Turin.

About an hour to the east of Turin sits La Casaccia, where some of my best—and worst—experiences on a bike took place. When I saw that my hosts had electric bikes, my eyes lit up! It meant that I could cover much more of the surrounding hills. While one might not experience the satisfaction that comes from conquering hills under your own power, getting to see more of the countryside was a trade-off I was happy to make, or so I thought.

After instructions from Giovanni, I set out for my inaugural ride the day after arriving. I descended the hill from Cella Monte without difficulty, and from there began following a quiet road along the valley floor. Here is where it got ugly. While making a turn to read a road sign that I had missed, I pressed the pedal. What I had not grasped from Giovanni's tutorial was that electric bikes provide extra power the instant you start to pedal. Even at the lowest level, the power boost caused me to make a wider turn than expected, and I was in the ditch with the bike piled on top of me before I could blink. Though not hurt, I was stunned. What had happened?

To make matters worse, the concrete drainage ditch had prickly wet vines masking a three-foot drop. The covering was thick with bugs, but nature's cushion probably saved me from serious harm. I was able to push off the heavy bike and stand up, but there was no way I could lift it out of the ditch. After failed attempts to flag down passing cars, I managed to attract the attention of a man on a motorcycle. He was worried I was hurt. I was more concerned about the bike, fearing I may have to bring it back damaged. I brushed us both off, checked for any blood, or dents, and finding none, continued my ride. I hid the crazy rash on my arms for the next few days until all evidence was gone. Accident? What accident?

Unaware of my earlier escapades, Giovanni suggested I take the English-speaking B&B guests for a bike tour. Absolutely.

That was my kind of work. We headed towards the small town of Ottiglio, along a route I was reasonably familiar with at this point. We were craving a good cappuccino, but unfortunately the cafe was closed. I suggested heading up towards the castle, but after climbing towards the top of the hill I could see it was going to be a fruitless quest. A local confirmed that I would find no cafes in that area. I waited for the others—to no avail. Assuming they had opted not to climb the hill, I made my way back down to the closed cafe. Finding no sign of them, I called Margherita and sheepishly confessed that I had 'lost' our guests. The only option was to return home, which I did in double-quick time.

I spotted the couple as I arrived at the base of a hill below Cella Monte. What a relief. I learned that they had somehow managed to pass me—the stone wall that separated me from the road while I was stopped must have been the culprit. Assuming I had left them, which I certainly would not have done, they had followed their little map to get home. Their only real concern was a malfunctioning bike, but at least we were almost home.

Another challenging bike story comes from Sassari, in northwest Sardinia, where I had borrowed Rosanna's bike for a morning ride. I did have a game plan, and a mobile device, but I was still unable to find a route back across the main highway that separated me from home. Stubbornly not wanting to turn around and retrace my route, the only option, as I saw it, was to cut through a field (or several) that appeared to provide an alternative. I visualised a path that seemed simple enough, down into the valley and out the other side. This cross-country venture began well enough but eventually required climbing over a crumbling stone wall, bike in tow, and under a fence. Back home, I assured Rosanna that my ride was enjoyable. A girl is entitled to a few secrets.

Perhaps my most regrettable cycling experience occurred when we were in Tuscany with friends, visiting the Chianti wine area. The four of us decided to take a day off to relax around the pool at our villa; but first, a bike ride seemed in order. Gord doesn't ride much, but he decided to join me, and our friend Peter did as well. The frames of the available bikes were on the small side for us but were otherwise operational. In my much-needed defence, at one point I did stop to say that I was going to head down a steep path, and the others confirmed that they were on board. Now there was no turning back.

I had brought a mobile device, so I wouldn't get us lost, but that plan quickly disintegrated. I had programmed it to show walking routes (seemingly the only alternative available besides driving), which turned into washed-out paths and rocky country lanes that were virtually un-rideable. It wasn't too bad on the way down. After a forage through someone's yard, we found a young man clearing brush in an olive grove who, with his delightful Tuscan accent, satisfied me that there was hope. The land soon flattened out as we made our way to the valley floor, and things began looking more promising. We met a man working a grape press who told us a bit about the process and that the grapes were Trebbiano. I recognised the name—not surprising, as it is one of the most widely planted white wine grape varieties in the world. Further along, we stopped to refill our water bottles. Unfortunately, things went downhill from there, even though at this point we were heading back up.

Our options were to follow a longer route that we had taken in the car, or a shorter route that meant a steeper climb. Fatefully, we opted for the latter. It would have been a challenge even on properly fitted high-performance bikes, and ours were anything but. We pushed and pedalled, walking more than biking at times, and finally made it to a plateau where we got some short-lived relief. I blamed the technology but should have known better. My device continued to direct us to walking trails that became impassable on bikes. No one was happy. Gord had not been on a bike in years, and this was clearly not what he had signed up for. Also, his bike was too small, making it difficult to get any power on the rare occasion when the ground was solid enough to allow for it.

We all fell silent, focusing our energy on getting up the unforgiving trails. The path finally dumped us out onto the paved road we would have been on had we opted for the longer route, but there was still more climbing ahead. Eventually we dragged our sorry behinds back home, exhausted, with no energy to even begin to explain where the heck we'd been. That night I was not sharing my dolce with anyone.

Gord and Peter pushing their bikes up the
cypress-lined drive to Il Colle.

On a more cheerful note, I am grateful to Antonia, my Danish colleague, who I biked with on my last day at La Casaccia. We were heading to Vignale Monferrato, a quaint hilltop town, until our plans were kyboshed by a flat tire. She knew how keen I was to visit the town and that it would be my last chance to bike before I left, so she offered to exchange bicycles. Elena came and picked Antonia up and I was able to visit the town and continue my ride. What a sweetheart.

As film maker Werner Herzog is quoted as saying, when you travel on foot you are 'reading the world, learning the essence of the world'. I like to think that my travels by foot and by bicycle offered me an opportunity to do just that—allowing Italy's essence to open itself up to me more intimately, one step at a time.

CHAPTER 15

Mangia! Mangia! – Eat! Eat!

If you really want to make a friend, go to someone's house and eat with him ... the people who give you their food give you their heart.

—Cesar Chavez

I was not surprised to learn that the Slow Food movement grew out of Italy—an enterprise born in Piedmont to prevent the disappearance of local food cultures and traditions. Striving to preserve traditional and regional cuisine, the organisation supports local producers and sustainable foods and encourages the use of produce that is characteristic of the local ecosystem. Today the global movement involves thousands of projects in over 160 countries embracing 'a comprehensive approach to food that recognises the strong connections between plate, planet, people, politics, and culture'.

If you know nothing else about Italy, you know spaghetti and linguini, mozzarella and ricotta, and gelato and pizza of course. But what you know outside the country is often different from what you will find if you are lucky enough to visit this land of riches. Its obliging climate ensures that fresh, natural ingredients are available all over Italy: simple, locally grown produce that follows the seasons is the key to the quality of Italian food. Not only richer in nutrients, in-season produce just tastes better. The quality of ingredients available in the prairies of western Canada, for example, cannot compare.

Take the delightful little tomato. Years ago, a friend made a temporary move to Italy. When she returned, she tried to describe how different the tomatoes tasted. How they actually 'had some taste'. It was not until I travelled to Italy myself that I fully grasped what she meant. Unlike the imported tomatoes we frequently find in our grocery stores, Italian tomatoes are sweet and juicy.

I remember eating delicious little oblong-shaped tomatoes at Gatta Morena. I was told they were *pachino*, a type of cherry tomato from the Sicilian town of the same name; that you could tell by their shape. What? A town has its own tomato, and it is that famous? Apparently so. Perhaps not surprisingly, the municipality of Pachino has among the greatest number of sunlight hours in Europe. The area also has the advantage of brackish groundwater, owing to its proximity to the sea, which

Margherita and Antonia picking tomatoes at La Casaccia.

is absorbed by the plants and converted to sugar, giving these little gems their full, sweet taste.

Similarly, the San Marzano tomato originates from San Marzano sul Sarno, near Naples. It is one of only two varieties of tomato that can be used for 'true Neapolitan pizza', which helps explain why North American menus will often identify San Marzano in their pizza ingredients. They are considered premium paste tomatoes because the taste is stronger and sweeter, and less acidic than many other varieties.

I conducted my own research to determine why something that is passed off as a tomato in our local stores tasted nothing like those in Italy; sometimes like nothing at all. I learned that our tomatoes are designed to travel well and to look nice, but with little (if any) concern for taste. To be shipped long distances, they must be picked before they are ripe and above all must be durable. Hardly the characteristics of a prize-winning tomato. The result is something that may look like a tomato but barely tastes like one, and likely has few of the nutrients. Certainly, we have options to shop at local markets and organic stores or grow our own in the summer if we have the space, like my backyard urban farmer sister. But the organic vegetables we must seek out and pay higher prices for, especially during the winter, are at your fingertips in Italy.

The cuisine also has other advantages. While many countries have regional culinary traditions, the diversity is arguably more pronounced in Italy. Despite its relatively small size, Italy's varied terrain and long coastline account for strong regional differences. These variations were augmented by a succession of conquerors from different lands and influences from neighbouring countries, resulting in an incredible range of culinary dishes. The cuisine is also influenced by local history— since autonomous regions were not unified under the Italian flag until 1861, there is no such thing as 'Italian cuisine'.

Although there is no classic national cuisine or formalised haute cuisine (as in France, for example), the food of Italy is distinctively 'Italian', with its own flavours and characteristics. What we think of today as 'Italian cooking' is a combination of traditional peasant food and the elaborate food of noble families that has developed over centuries. Additionally, recipes evolve to suit modern tastes and preferences—such as more fish and vegetables, less meat and fats, fresher and lighter fare that is quick and easy to prepare.

In her book, *The Food of Italy*, Claudia Roden notes that mass migration of Italians from south to north and other factors have complicated the picture in terms of the delineation of culinary borders. Prior to World War II, for example, Roden notes that the country could be divided based on two main food groups: fats and carbohydrates. In northern Italy butter was used, and the carbohydrates of choice were rice and polenta. By contrast, cooking in the south centred around olive oil, pasta, and pizza (using tomatoes for everything). Now, pizza and pasta are everywhere.

That said, regional cuisines have managed to survive, as I saw first-hand. In the north, at places like La Casaccia and in the mountains of Aosta Valley, I ate risotto and polenta more than pasta, breads were often mixed-grain and heavier, and sauces tended to be creamy rather than tomato-y. In central and southern Italy, pizza and pasta still reign, and most dishes use olive oil, garlic, and tomatoes.

Sicilian cuisine, on the other hand, is in a world of its own. It features some of the most exotic and colourful cooking in Italy, evidence of the many cultures that have existed on the island over its history. The Phoenicians introduced the use of salt in the curing and preserving of fish and other foods; Greeks brought honey and wine, as well as olives, ricotta cheese and *focaccia*; the Byzantines introduced sharp cheeses and spicy biscuits; the Normans introduced salted cod (*baccala*); and the Spanish brought cocoa and tomato sauce (tomatoes actually came to Italy from North America via Spanish traders).

Relics of the Arab civilisation include couscous (*cuscusu*) with fish, stuffed vegetables, and prolific use of oranges, lemons, pistachios, almonds, and even pasta (Sicily is the oldest location in Italy where records indicate the use of pasta). You will also see (and smell) spices such as saffron, nutmeg, cloves, and cinnamon that are commonly used (versus more herbs elsewhere in Italy).

Italian food products have a strict labelling system designed to protect regional products from lower quality versions. A DOP designation translates to Protected Designation of Origin and guarantees a product came from a specific location and was produced using traditional methods. Common examples include prosciutto di Parma (cured ham from Parma), parmigiano reggiano (cheese made in Parma and Reggio Emilia), aceto balsamico di Modena (balsamic vinegar of Modena), and San Marzano tomatoes, discussed above. The IGP designation translates to Protected Geographic Zone, an equally important designation although the rules are not as strict.

To understand just how particular the standards are, we can consider parmigiano reggiano. Each step of the cheese-making process must be tracked, down to the location where the cows live, where their feed comes from, and where and how the cheese is produced. A cow that eats crops from outside the DOP area may cause the milk to taste different and therefore affect the taste of the final product. So, when you see a green canister of 'parmesan cheese' in the supermarket, it may appear Italian, but this rebranded version is nothing like the original. Unfortunately, knockoffs are a popular way to take advantage of identifiable, high-quality Italian products, whether Gucci bags or cheese.

I think it's fair to say that Italians have a healthier relationship with their food than is generally the case in North

America. Everywhere I spent time, locals I met seemed to have an innate appreciation of the food of their area—what was local and in season, specialty dishes that date back generations, the many varieties of cheese produced locally, keys to great olive oil and tomato sauce, how to make the lightest pizza dough with reduced gluten, how to make limoncello and a range of other homemade liqueurs. The list goes on. Below are stories that I hope demonstrate this connection to the simple foods of Italy that offer a culturally rich cuisine.

Pasta

The history of pasta is unclear. According to a popular legend, Marco Polo introduced pasta to Italy in the thirteenth century following his travels in the Far East. This theory is plausible, given that the Chinese have apparently been eating noodles since 3000 BC, but there is also evidence that the Etruscans were already eating pasta by this time. Regardless of its origin, it remains a staple of the Italian diet, served in a large array of shapes and sizes depending on the dish.

Many classic Italian dishes today are built around the simple country food of the peasants and farmers who used inexpensive and readily available items such as legumes, pasta, and the leftover bits of animals. Nothing went to waste. *Pasta e fagioli* (pasta and bean soup) is one such example of the *cucina povera*, traditionally considered a poor man's food. Legumes replaced expensive meats and the pasta helped fill bellies. There are many variations of this soup, which is popular throughout Italy.

My first experience with *pasta e fagioli* was in Canada at Joe's parents' home, when our soccer group was invited for dinner. Joe's dad did the cooking, as he always did, while his mom sat and questioned every move. It was quite comical. With a twinkle in his eye, Luigi took it all in stride. The process was laborious, starting from the straining of tomatoes and boiling of vegetables to flavour the broth. No store-bought broth or tomato sauce here. When we finally sat down to eat, the quantity and assortment of food was overwhelming. An invitation for pasta and bean soup turned into a multi-course meal.

This was my first experience eating at the home of Italians. I have since learned not to fill up on *il primo* (the first plate, often pasta), because there is much more to come. I also recall bowls of leftover pasta that got dished out for everyone to take home. I didn't know this dish beforehand, but by the time we had finished our leftovers I knew it well.

Pici is a thick rustic spaghetti, a specialty of Tuscany. I watched our host make it at the villa we had rented in southern Tuscany. It was the first course in a meal she prepared for our group. I know there is a great deal of technique to making good, melt-in-your-mouth pasta, but she made it look easy. Make a well in the middle of a pile of flour, add a couple of eggs, and incorporate them into the surrounding flour to form a dough; then knead it, rest it, roll it, cut it into long thin strips and shape them between your hands. *Finito*. Done. Kidding aside, I was happy to sit back and enjoy the fruits of her labour.

Travelling on my own one summer, I rented a car in Apulia for a day trip to the city of Matera, in the southern region of Basilicata (located between the toe and heel of the Italian boot, with coasts along both the Tyrrhenian and Ionian Seas). Matera is known for its Sassi District, a vast hillside complex of cave dwellings carved into the ancient river canyon. The caves date back thousands of years, the area cited as one of the oldest continuously inhabited cities in the world. By the late 1800s, the dwellings were noted for abject poverty, poor sanitation, and rampant disease. An embarrassment, the government finally evacuated the residents to more modern housing in 1952, after which the *sassi* lay vacant until the 1980s. With renewed interest, the area has become a tourism destination and vibrant arts community, with old dwellings converted into hotels, museums, and restaurants. UNESCO named the Sassi District a World Heritage Site in 1993.

After finishing my walking tour around this unique town, I found a spot for a late lunch and took the opportunity to try the classic *orecchietti con cime di rapa*—little ear-shaped pasta shells with broccoli rabe (also known as rapini). I don't routinely eat pasta, and found the dish heavy for my tastes, but I was glad I had experimented with it. While enjoying my lunch I struck up a conversation with a young Roman couple beside me. They spoke clear Italian that I was able to understand and I was pleased when they complimented my Italian. Yes, this is a recurring theme, if you haven't noticed; I remember anyone who praises my Italian! This was when I was still very much learning the language and I welcomed any encouragement I could get.

While staying with an Italian friend's mother on another occasion, she made a similar pasta. It was also memorable, but for different reasons. When I asked for the salt, her response made me pause. Speaking Italian, she said that I could add salt if I wanted, but that in her opinion *è perfetto cosi* (it is perfect the way it is). To me, her response reflected how seriously Italians take their food. I did not add any salt, by the way.

I tried a local favourite, *pasta trapanese*, in the northwest corner of Sicily, and was hooked. Corkscrew-shaped *busiate* pasta is used in this dish, together with Trapani pesto, both typical of the area. The pesto is believed to have originated from the famous Genovese pesto (Genoa is in northern Liguria) but with modifications to take advantage of local ingredients, such as almonds and tomatoes. Depending on taste, it may also include grated cheese, chili peppers, or

Maria

toasted breadcrumbs. Like my pizza margherita in Naples, it is one of those meals I keep coming back to when I think about the best of the best.

You heard a bit about Maria earlier. Here she is serving up a huge bowl of spaghetti at a meal we shared with her family in the small town of Delia, on the island of Sicily. The pasta was delicious, and that smile of hers contagious.

Pizza

Sampling traditional local fare as you travel offers a lesson in an area's culture and history. Ingredients will be seasonal and local, spices and cooking processes revealing ethnicity and cultural customs. Pizza is no exception. The history of pizza, or similar types of food, has been traced back around 10,000 years to the Neolithic period, when people began adding various ingredients to bread to make it more flavourful. More recently, if you can call it that, records reveal Persian soldiers baking flatbread topped with cheese and dates in the sixth century BC and ancient Greeks adding oils, herbs, and cheese to theirs.

Modern pizza is similar. It may look different depending where your travels take you but is arguably one of the world's favourite comfort foods. Seasonings will also vary depending on what is commonly used in local cuisine. More unusual toppings can range from peanuts and bananas in Sweden to water chestnuts and peapods in China.

The history of pizza and international differences in topping choice notwithstanding, the debate in Italy over the best pizza tends to focus on Rome versus Naples. The main difference between the two is the dough. In Rome olive oil is added, which allows the dough to stretch more and thus create thinner, crispier pizzas. In Naples, the final product is still thin by North American standards, but it tends to be softer and easier to fold than its Roman counterpart. You are also more likely to find *pizza bianco* (white pizza, using oil instead of tomato sauce) in Rome than in Naples, where tomatoes and tomato-based sauces rule.

Unlike Rome, where there is not a stringent set of rules that every pizzeria must follow, Neapolitan pizza is strictly regulated. A pizzeria must be certified by the 'pizza police' to ensure precise standards are met before it can call its pizza Neapolitan. Ingredients must include only specific tomatoes from the Naples area and only certified mozzarella di bufala (mozzarella made from the creamy white milk of water buffalo).

UNESCO began protecting 'diverse cultural practices and creative expressions' in 2008, and the art of Neapolitan pizza-making (*pizzaiolo*) was added to this list in 2017. The honour was awarded not only for its taste and technique, but also for the process, characterised as a spectacle 'that fosters social gatherings and intergenerational exchange between pizza makers and their customers as they demonstrate their pie-making skills'. As the acclaimed home of pizza, Naples even has an eleven-day festival to celebrate this classic dish. That, I need to fit into my next Italian adventure.

One does not go to Italy without consuming significant quantities of pizza over the years, but certain spots stand out. My best memory remains a simple and inexpensive pizza margherita (the archetype of Neapolitan pizza) in the streets of Naples on a rainy soccer Sunday. I have been searching for something as unforgettable ever since, to no avail, though I certainly have not suffered in the process.

I recall my father trying to find a place for us to eat pizza in Milan when I was there with him as a youngster. We were told to come back later, at 7:00 p.m. I believe it was. As a rule, restaurants don't even start serving dinner until 8:00 p.m. When you understand Italian rituals and eating habits it makes sense, but for us it was confusing. How could we not find somewhere to eat pizza, in Italy?

Something similar happened at a place tucked away in the hills above Salerno, south of Naples on the Amalfi Coast. Our B&B host suggested a nearby restaurant. Gord and I arrived just before 8 p.m. to find no one in sight. Eventually a young man came out, graciously seated us, and brought out glasses of prosecco and a small plate of cheese and olives to tide us over. People started arriving around 8:30 p.m. and just kept coming, filling the entire large outdoor terrace by the time we had finished eating. Evidently it was a favourite spot for pizza, and even though it was a Sunday night, families with young children remained well into the evening.

One pizza meal in Fondi came with the bonus of the owner bringing out his guitar to serenade us. More recently our go-to place there has been the popular Zio Mario's Pizzeria, and not just because of the pizza. We struck up a conversation with the owner's son on our first visit, and the next thing we knew he was bringing us samples of his mom's antipasti from the kitchen. On at least two other occasions we had interesting conversations with a local artist who was a regular. His sculptures are on display around Fondi. As we watched customers stream in and out, often taking an armload of pizza to go, it seemed like everyone was family. Taking the opportunity to strike up conversations as we did, went a long way to making us feel a small part of that family a well.

My craziest pizza experience was in a small town called Vallecorsa, in the Ausoni Mountains of Lazio. We went with friends, on their recommendation. Owned by a couple from Sorrento, a few hours to the south, they ran their pizzeria four days a week, and then returned home in between. I'm not sure how they ended up in this small mountain town, but apparently it was worth the commute. The six of us started with two enormous platters of antipasti. I could have called it a night right then, but we still had pizza to come. At this establishment, pizza is ordered by the metre. I now know just how much pizza that is. After each of us listed the toppings we wanted, we ended up with two massive pizzas. It was crazy, especially after the appetizers. The couple also make their own limoncello, a digestive, which we all were happy to accept after that meal. The pizza was delicious, but next time we will know to skip the antipasti!

Pizza is a very personal thing, but in Italy you will find a thinner crust, fewer toppings, and lighter on the *formaggio* than the loaded North American versions tend to be. Fortunately, there are fine pizzaioli right here in Alberta, so I don't have to wait for a return trip to Italy to enjoy a good pizza. But my most memorable experiences will always be the ones shared with friends in Italy.

Pane – Bread

In North America, bread tends to be used as a vehicle for sandwiches, or to accompany saucy pasta dishes, rather than as a delicious food on its own. In Italy, the opposite is often true. Bread is meant to be eaten with food and is considered an important aspect of a meal. The exception is starchy meals such as pasta; Italians generally don't even eat bread with pasta because both are starches. Please note that it is also un-Italian to eat bread as an appetizer on its own while waiting for your meal, and especially if you ask for olive oil and balsamic vinegar to dip it in. It is just not Italian to fill up on bread before dinner.

An exception might be where the bread is toasted and drizzled with olive oil or other *bruschetta* toppings (pronounce the '*che*' like a 'k'), as this is an antipasto rightly eaten before your pasta course. Another exception is focaccia, a light, pizza-like bread that is eaten as a snack on its own. Italians also have delicious recipes to use up stale bread, like Tuscan panzanella. I mentioned trying a variation of this in Lazio that included chickpeas. The Tuscan version is a thick salad, where tomatoes and olive oil soften the stale bread.

While there are national staples, such as *ciabatta* bread (a rustic bread made from sticky wet dough that creates a porous, chewy texture and unique taste), you will always find local varieties. In Fondi, for example, bread from the nearby town of Campodimele is popular, and people would routinely ask for it by name; and we would ask for *rosette*, named after the shape of these little buns, when we wanted to make sandwiches for the beach. Tuscan bread is traditionally made without salt. This practice is said to date back to the Middle Ages when salt was a prized (and therefore expensive) commodity. The solution for impoverished Tuscans was to make bread without it. Since bread is intended to be eaten with meals, the missing salt was made up for in the meal. As mentioned, the park ranger's *pane carasau* in Sardinia was more like crackers than bread. Not my favourite, but it serves a purpose. At La Casaccia, I learned about *pasta madre* or 'mother dough', a sourdough bread starter that is used widely across Italy. With less gluten, it is easier to digest than conventional bread. Elena had a starter that has been growing for over twenty years. A woman from Holland was leaving the day after I arrived, and she was taking a sample of Elena's starter with her. The tradition goes international.

Here is a cute story to end this section. While making our way through the rugged interior of Abruzzo, we stopped for a break in a small town near Lake Barrea. As I poked around the shops along main street, I walked by a *panificio* (bakery). Inside was an older man at work, managing large round loaves on a long paddle he was using to reach into the oven. From experience I knew there are many types of bread in Italy, with all sorts of names. So, when I asked the baker what type of bread he was making, I was taken by surprise over his simple response of *pane*—like what other type is there?

The baker who said his *pane* is called *pane*.

No Formaggio sul Pesce – No Cheese on the Fish

Early on in my travels, I learned that Italians do not eat cheese with their fish. Like drinking red wine with fish, or a caffè latte after an evening meal, it is frowned upon at best. Depending where you eat, you may get more than a frown. We were dining in a small restaurant in the Spanish quarter of Naples once, where a table of tourists had ordered pasta with seafood. When their meals arrived, someone asked for grated cheese. The owner's response was clear—*no formaggio sul pesce*. The diners insisted, but she was equally adamant.

Perhaps I should have included this ritual in the section on the chiesa, as Italians are deeply religious about mixing cheese and fish or seafood. Many will explain that cheese can overpower the more delicate flavour of fish. Others find this explanation nonsensical, since there is seafood that has a strong flavour (such as clams, oysters, and sardines) and cheeses that are quite mild (such as ricotta and mozzarella). Others claim that it just does not taste good. Whatever the reason, the prohibition is ancient and entrenched, even though one can find recipes from around the world that successfully combine the two. And even in Italy, perhaps because it is Italy, there are exceptions.

I have read about exceptions such as pizza with anchovies, which I know is a favourite in the south. My personal experience occurred in a seaside restaurant in Vieste, on the Gargano promontory of Apulia. At the recommendation of our B&B host, I ordered *cozze ripiene* (stuffed mussels). The delicious Pugliese recipe included not one but two types of cheese: ricotta and parmigiano. You can find similar recipes in the Maremma area of southern Tuscany/northern Lazio. This area has a long coastline, where fish and seafood are often the centrepiece of dishes. The area is also noted for its cheese production, particularly pecorino and ricotta. Because of the local emphasis on fish and cheese, it is less surprising that Maremma recipes might incorporate both.

For the record, I love cheese sprinkled on my seafood pasta and have no qualms asking for it (hoping of course that I won't be shamed in the process). I would not order cheese with a straight seafood dish, but when the two are mixed, I need my parmigiano. It is good to know that I fit into the exception to the rule at least.

Pitigliano is a scenic medieval town in Tuscany, dramatically situated above a steep river valley. It is part of an area called Borghi del Tufo where towns have been built from the surrounding volcanic tuff rock. The town was known as Little Jerusalem, being a haven for a large Jewish community from as early as the fourteenth century. It was later made up largely of people fleeing persecution in Rome during World War II. The old town is attractively lit at night, and we intentionally stayed late one evening to dine at a restaurant with a captivating view of the lights across the valley. Here we had an interesting chat with the Neapolitan owner who ran the place with his wife. We were assured that Italians do not put cheese on their *pesce*. There was clearly no middle ground for them, so we left it at that.

I learned a useful fact about seafood early in my travels, though there is no cheese involved in this story. We had taken the ferry across the Gulf of Naples, from Sorrento to Capri, and on the way back I was enjoying practising my Italian with a local as my victim. I was unfamiliar with the term *mare mosso* or 'red tide', but I got the gist of what he was saying—it was not a good time to eat mussels. I later learned that 'red tide' is a term for algae blooms, a concentration of aquatic microorganisms that can be harmful when ingested. A red tide is more common during rough seas (mare mosso), which was the case when we were returning from Capri. Point taken.

Dolce – Dessert

Although there are certain desserts that may be found throughout Italy, and even internationally (*tiramisu* quickly comes to mind), Italian dolce recipes are typically more regional—or even local—specialties. I am a self-confessed *dolce afficionado* (if that means I like to eat dessert) and have happily tried many variations across Italy, but a few experiences are particularly memorable.

When it comes to dessert, I left my heart on Elba Island, where I fell in love with *torta caprese*. To be clear, I am talking about a cake, not a caprese salad with tomatoes and mozzarella. The name comes from the island of Capri, where this decadent chocolate cake was first created. Its ingredients include chopped or ground almonds instead of flour, fluffy egg whites instead of baking powder, and rich dark chocolate. I shared my first piece, but after one bite there was no question—I would be ordering a full piece for myself next time. I tried to find it again in Siena, even stopping at a local bakery to inquire. The woman had no idea what I was talking about. It was another indication of how local a recipe can be. Back in Canada, I could not forget my new favourite dolce. I found recipes on the internet, including one by Italian Canadian chef David Rocco, that I have been using for special occasions ever since. I am not a baker, but even I can do justice to this simple *ricetta*.

I found another unexpected pleasure in Stintino, a seaside town in northern Sardinia. While walking along the marina, I spotted an advertisement for something called *seada*, a lightly fried pastry with a melted cheese filling, covered with a drizzle of honey and slice of orange. Fried food generally does not appeal to me, but I wanted to taste this local treat. It was crispy but light, the sweetness well balanced by the gooey cheese. It was an exception to fried food that I would make again.

In Cefalù I ordered *cassata*, a traditional dessert from Sicily. I wanted to try it before leaving the island but was surprised by what I was served. I knew cassata from an Italian Canadian friend, her version made with layers of different-flavoured ice cream that included candied fruit. Here I was presented with a piece of cake layered with candied fruit and decorated with pink and green icing. Although quite different desserts, I would never turn down either.

Baci, made by the chocolate confectionery company Perugina, are chocolate 'kisses' filled with a chocolate and hazelnut mixture and wrapped in a multilingual love note. I was familiar with these little delights, always reading the love notes in Italian first to see if I could figure out what they said before checking the English translation. But I did not know the history behind the love note tradition until talking to a couple at Parco di Vulci (an Etruscan-Roman Archaeological Park in northern Lazio). The woman mentioned that she was from Perugia, in Umbria, a land-locked region in the heart of Italy and the home of Perugina chocolates. I responded that I had enjoyed visiting her hometown and sampling the chocolates. She then shared how the love notes had come to be. As the story goes, a young lady who had fallen in love with a founder of the chocolate company would wrap romantic notes around special bite-size chocolates that she made for him. And nearly one hundred years later, the tradition continues.

To close this chapter, here is a fun story from our ridiculously cute assistant at a marina in Scarlino. After a week of sailing off the coast of Tuscany, we returned to the marina and prepared for the inspection of our chartered boat. I mentioned to this tiny gal that we had dropped a jar of Nutella into the storage area. She instantly hopped down into the compact space and surfaced with the jar, and a smile. Nutella is apparently near and dear to her heart too. She confessed to consuming a kilogram per week. *Mi scusi?* I love Nutella, but use it as a treat, not a main course. However, if this tiny thing could eat so much of it without gaining weight, maybe I needed to rethink my strategy.

For those not familiar with Nutella, it is a hazelnut and chocolate paste that Italians love to spread on bread or inject into croissants and other pastries. Now world-famous, it was developed in the Piedmont region during the Napoleonic wars when there was an English embargo on cacao. The region's abundant hazelnuts became an effective alternative.

CHAPTER 16

Amici e Famiglia – Friends and Family

The best part of life is when your family become you friends and your friends become your family.
—Robin Roberts

I was going to write a chapter about family and another about friends, but it proved impossible to separate the two. So, you will find interwoven stories about both. I introduced you to some of these people and places earlier, but here I want to honour those who have helped me discover the real Italy. My love for Italy is wrapped up in my love for them. They are my friends, and my extended Italian family.

Italy is an incredibly diverse country, as we have seen. But a common denominator is their love of, and reliance on, family. My experience of the Italian extended family shed light on a way of life that nurtures individuals within the group and sustains a healthy society. Family is at the heart of the Italian culture and way of life. Circumstances differ for everyone, but Italians generally have extended family around them, if not living with them.

Perhaps this left a greater impression on me because I did not experience family in the same way as a youth. My parents were from Scotland and Hungary, I was a first generation Canadian, and we had no relatives in Canada. Although we visited both countries on occasion, it was impossible to connect with extended family members the way one might without an ocean divide. I never met my grandmothers. I barely knew my grandfathers, who both died when I was young. I was lucky to cross paths with my Scottish cousins when we visited Scotland, but I met one set of Australian cousins only once. I was five. I met another Australian cousin at my wedding, when he was a baby; his sister not until we were adults.

We could have done more to reach out, but it was a challenge. I would write occasional letters to my step-grandmother, to thank her for a birthday or Christmas present, but there was no email or FaceTime conversations back then. Letters would travel by snail mail, leaving me wondering if they had even arrived. After my step-grandmother's death, my mom was forwarded a couple of sweet letters that I had written as a child. It was meaningful that she had kept them. As for my nuclear family, it is spread across Canada, my mom's family across at least three continents, my father's in Hungary.

None of this is right or wrong, just a note about how it was. I can contrast it with my husband's farming family; his siblings still all live in the same city and grew up knowing all four grandparents. It isn't that families are necessarily disconnected in Canada, just that the same connections were not there for mine. The miles distanced us, though, happily, we seem to be making up for lost time as adults.

I can also contrast what I grew up understanding about family with Joe and Filomena's Italian Canadian family, to take an example. Their daughters and grandchildren all have lived in the same city since birth, the grandkids growing up with each other and having their grandparents involved in their lives. They even had their *bisnonna* (great-grandmother) with them while growing up. Gord and I have been blessed to be welcomed into their home, to meet their children and grandchildren, and to witness the dynamics and celebrations of their extended Italian family.

The definition of family is arguably murky at best. In the traditional western context, family is defined as a group of people related by blood or marriage. Brothers and sisters, aunts and uncles, parents and grandparents, husbands and wives. But we can no longer rely on this simplistic definition. In the modern context, this description has been blown wide open as the make-up of the various combinations of relationships that call themselves a family continues to evolve, and as society continues to acknowledge and accept these growing definitions of a family unit. In fact, current definitions of family speak to a much more subjective meaning that focuses not on blood lines and DNA but on the intimacy of relationships built on love, compassion, and support.

As I read about how family and friendship are defined, it seemed that one could easily substitute for the other. Friendship is seen as a relationship of mutual affection, and although it can manifest in different ways from place to place, the characteristics of friendship are similar everywhere—affection and kindness, sympathy and compassion, mutual understanding and forgiveness, and the ability to be oneself without fear of judgement. Is this not looking remarkably like the modern perspective on family?

When family is geographically distant and friends are close, or when we get the love and support from our friends that is absent in our family relationships, it is not surprising that we seek to build our lives around those friendships. And in Italy, a place where I have no family, this is exactly what occurred in my case. The Italians I met treat a cousin's cousin like one of their own, and good friends as part of their family. Even if I was just a friend of a friend, I was embraced as a friend of theirs as well.

Thanks in large part to Joe and Filomena, we now have a family of friends in Italy. Their stories are at the real heart of Italy for me. I met many people over the years who were interesting, helpful, fun, passionate, kind, and memorable. But here I want to shine a light on those who transformed Italy for me, and really, who transformed me. They enabled me to peer inside Italy as more than just a tourist gazing up at the Sistine Chapel. It has been a heart-opening experience. I also hope you will see my friends in people you meet on your travels. There are special people everywhere. Your choice is to open yourself up to them, and they will do the same for you.

Fondi, Lazio – Home Away From Home

Fondi is the hometown of my friend Joe F, a small city about 90 minutes south of Rome. Fondi's early history predates the Romans and is also later linked to that of the Roman Empire. For over 2,000 years prior to the construction of more modern infrastructure between Rome and Naples, Fondi was an important settlement along the ancient Via Appia, the main transportation route from Rome to much of southern Italy. Restored portions of the Via Appia can be found along Corso Appio Claudio in the heart of Fondi's historic centre, as well as south of the city. Remaining Roman ruins include portions of ancient city walls and Roman baths uncovered near the fortress (called Castello Caetani). There is even some evidence of walls constructed using Cyclopean masonry which dates to the seventh century BC.

Joe's family of four arrived in Canada in 1964, having set sail from Naples nine days earlier. While they had a good life in Fondi, his father Luigi was looking for something more. Friends and relatives made the trek from Fondi to see the family off, thanks to a bus chartered by Joe's parents. I'm told there were lots of tears, but well wishes and excitement too. Several years later, Joe met Filomena, his wife-to-be, whose family had immigrated to Canada as well. We have had belly laughs hearing their stories, including how they could not go anywhere together without a chaperone. The only solution—marriage. Fil was young, but she knew Joe was the one. And three children and six grandchildren later, *la vita è bella*.

I met Joe through soccer, a life-long passion of his. And from there, Gord and I met Fil and their family. We also got to know several of their Italian Canadian friends in Edmonton, as well as younger Italian newcomers whom we now call friends as well. These relationships exposed me to the Italian lifestyle, including their focus on family, and food of course. This too has been part of my journey. We have shared Christmas dinner with their family, joined them and their Italian friends for celebrations over copious amounts of food, belted out Italian songs to karaoke machines, or with Joe on guitar around the fire, and laughed endlessly.

My love of Fondi started years ago, when we were first invited to stay with Joe and Fil in their family home. The oppressive heat in the earlier years was a challenge, as was the humidity. I'd never experienced anything like it. On my first visit, Gord, my brother, and I stayed in one large room, and I for one did not get much sleep. Over the years, as the family used the house more, ceiling fans and air conditioners were added, making life much more comfortable. We adapt when we need to, but this soft Canadese was happy she didn't have to adapt for too long. We have visited many times since and have met several family members, including Joe's aunt and uncle who lived upstairs. Zia Gina is still in their home, although Zio Paulo has sadly passed. Over the years we also met some of their friends, who you will hear more about.

The Feula family in Fondi (2008), with Filomena
and Joe standing, Zia Gina, Joes mom Leondina,
Zio Paulo, and Joe's dad Luigi seated.

With the close quarters of most Italian cities, Fondi included,
it is impossible not to know your neighbours, sometimes more
intimately than you care to. This aspect of Italian 'street life',
which I saw, and heard, play out around me, is one of my earliest
impressions of Italy. I would often see someone sitting on a step,
cell phone at their ear, frequently with a cigarette dangling
between their fingers, trying to have a private conversation.
With extended families living together in small spaces, there
was often more privacy outside than in. On occasion we would
be woken to the piercing screams of a distraught wife in a
couple's row, the realities of life spilling into the streets.

Even the laundry hanging in the streets told a story. It was all
part of the charm for me; everyone connected to everyone, whether
through family arguments or personal conversations enacted in
the streets, or their undergarments hanging for everyone to see.
And while I'm sure the charm wears thin when you experience it
daily, it is part of the pulse of life that attracted me to Italy.

While Fondi has its own charm, nearby Sperlonga stands out. It is a picturesque seaside village south of Fondi, perched on a promontory above a sandy coastline that goes on for miles. The name derives from the Latin *spelunca* (cave, grotto) after the natural sea caves shaping the coastline. The area was a favourite summer retreat for wealthy Romans, including Emperor Tiberius. The Emperor maintained an impressive villa here that included one of these grottos, aptly named Tiberius Cave. The cave can be accessed with admission to the nearby Sperlonga Archaeolgical Museum, which includes a display of ancient sculptures from the grounds of the former villa. I was more attracted by the beautiful views from the grotto, back along the beach to Sperlonga.

Originally settled as early as 10,000 BC, Sperlonga is now home to a white-washed entanglement of narrow streets and stairways, interspersed with characteristic cafes and restaurants. Unexpected views of the coastline also add to the allure. In the historic centre you will find a courtyard decorated with murals depicting Saracen and other invaders from the town's turbulent past.

A beach walk near Sperlonga.

Another nearby city that I have enjoyed showing friends and family around is Gaeta, located on a peninsula that juts out into the Tyrrhenian Sea south of Sperlonga. The city features a medieval centre that was protected by a massive fortress. The original castle was built in the late thirteenth century, with its fortification enhanced over its history. The fortress's varied uses included refuge for Pope Pius IX during an uprising of Italian nationalists in the late 1800s. A portion of the fortress was also used as a military prison until as recently as 1980. At the peninsula's summit is Monte Orlando, covered by a protected natural park with many trails running through it and down to the old town. I have hiked up here numerous times and the area has much to offer, including sea views, ruins of military fortifications dating back centuries, and a well preserved, first-century mausoleum.

The lower portion of the west side of the peninsula is known as Montagna Spaccata. The origins of the three deep crevices in the mountain are a source of religious legend, but it is an intriguing place whatever your beliefs. The area includes a sanctuary dedicated to the Holy Trinity and one of the crevices has a huge boulder suspended in it, upon which the tiny Cappella del Ss. Crocifisso (Chapel of the Crucifix) was built. You can also descend a steep set of stairs in another deep crevice that leads to Grotta del Turco (Turk's Grotto), once used as a hiding place by Turkish pirates.

A humorous story from Gaeta involved a friend from Canada. We had spent the morning walking around Monte Orlando, wandering through the streets of the old town, and then climbing up to the gates of the castle only to find it closed to tourists. Getting brave with my Italian, I asked if it was possible to have a quick look. *Aspetta*, the guard said. Wait here. A second man was sent inside, and a third individual appeared shorty after. He spoke a few words of

English, but the discussion was primarily in Italian. We were offered a tour, which I found quite surprising. I couldn't imagine why he was prepared to go out of his way to show us around but was not about to object. My friend had no idea what he was saying as he pointed to war exhibits and showed us the prison cells, but I did my best to translate what I could. Eventually we were led up to the roof of the massive structure, which rewarded us with an incredible view over the Bay of Gaeta.

I asked if he would take our picture. *Certo*, he responded. Then the table turned. Our guide asked if he could get his picture taken with my friend, and her contact information as well. Ah! It was all coming together. He was clearly infatuated. The question now was how to politely extricate ourselves from this prickly situation. We thanked him for his kindness and made our exit as quickly as we could get him to show us back to the gate. Wendy and I had a good laugh over lunch. Joe's nose was slightly out of joint (in a good-humoured way of course) when I told him the story. Hometown boy had been to the fortress with his soccer academy the year before and was refused access. He will just have to bring a pretty lady along next time.

I'm trying to think back on life in Fondi over the years, originally staying with Joe and Filomena, and for the last couple of years renting a nearby apartment where we quickly settled into the relaxing Mediterranean lifestyle. In short, I love how simple life is when I'm there, and I love taking part in the daily rituals. But more than anything, I love the experiences I've had there with special people I am blessed to call friends.

Double date with Joe and Filomena in Sperlonga.

B&B Gatta Morena, Lazio

Gatta Morena is a B&B in the rolling hills near Lazio's northern border with Tuscany. It is in the heart of ancient Etruscan territory and surrounded by the bubbling, mineral-rich waters that feed natural thermal springs. In under an hour, you can reach the Tyrrhenian Sea to the west and Lake Bolsena to the east, Viterbo to the south (one of the best-preserved medieval towns in central Italy), Monte Amiato to the north (a large lava dome of an ancient volcano and home to several ski resorts), and many Etruscan towns in between.

When I first visited this off-the-beaten-path B&B, the rustic villa was owned by Pino and Tiziana, who lived on the main level, and Elio who lived in an apartment above. Together they worked the land, using organic techniques to grow fruits, vegetables, nuts, and rows of lavender. They lived off the land as much as possible, reusing or recycling everything. They were well ahead of the curve in terms of sustainable living.

Elio had chucked life as an insurance adjuster in Rome to move to Gatta Morena. When I met him, his humble ambition was to care for the earth and be of service. I recall Elio describing his job in the streets of Rome. He would be called to a car accident to negotiate a settlement between the two parties, right there and then, thus avoiding the cost of lawyers and courts. Have you seen the traffic in Rome? The narrow streets and the craziness? And the vehicles? On more than one occasion I've noticed car bumpers strapped together using plastic zip-ties. I am quite sure he earned his money. And I can also see how someone of his nature would need to get out of there.

I was introduced to Gatta Morena following a sailing trip with my brother and our Fondi friends. We had been cruising around Elba Island, enjoying morning swims in pretty bays and delicious lunches, 'alla Filomena', on deck. In the evening we would tie up in a marina and walk around town before settling in for dinner somewhere, if not back on board. In addition to Fil's amazing cooking, memorable moments included taking a 'chairlift' up to Monte Capanne, the highest point on the island. The lift was barely more than a bird cage, holding two of us at a time while standing, but the views up top were worth the precarious ride.

I'm reminded of a similar experience on the Island of Capri. From Anacapri, the smaller of two towns on the island, there is a single chairlift that takes passengers to the top of Monte Solaro. It glides just above the fields below, and at the top you need to almost run off the lift or you will be heading right back down again. Once our feet were firmly planted, we were offered wonderful views, including down to Capri's famous *faraglioni*—rock stacks eroded over time by the constant slapping of waves and the blowing wind.

Back to Monte Capanne. Have you ever sat atop a mountain, or gazed out over the ocean with no horizon in sight, and felt like the world was so enormous and yet so intimate and small at the same time? That is how I felt up there. Standing on a large platform that dropped away like an infinity pool made me feel like the world itself was infinite and that I was a tiny part of something so much bigger than myself. It made me appreciate the depth and breadth of the beauty surrounding me and, simultaneously, made me feel closer connections with those around me, my husband, my brother, and our dear friends. It all felt surreal. I did not want to leave.

Atop Monte Capanne.

I was uncomfortable writing these words, wondering if anyone would understand. I wasn't even sure I fully understood. Then, absolutely by coincidence, I discovered the answer. I had randomly clicked on one of Oprah's podcasts, and she seemed to be talking about precisely what I was floundering to express. She understood! Her conversation was with a Dr. Alan Lightman, and the two were sharing experiences that sounded exactly like mine. The details of their stories were different, but the sentiment was the same. We are all part of something much greater than ourselves. That, I know for sure (as Oprah would say)!

A few days later we returned to the mainland and headed back to Fondi. This is when Gatta Morena came into the picture. Our friends knew the owners, and our group had been invited for lunch. An eclectic collection of Tiziana's friends were staying at the B&B when we arrived. Despite the language barrier, I felt welcome and connected instantly. We dined family-style at a large wooden table sheltered from the sun by a fragrant jasmine-covered pergola. It was an experience I would not forget—full of laughter among friends, and simple but delicious food.

Lunch at Gatta Morena, with Tiziana, Gord and SB
standing, Tiziana's friend and my brother seated.

The experience was also pivotal in my subsequent travels, which included other stays at Gatta Morena and long-term connections with people I met there. The initial visit was short, but I felt an innate sense of tranquility and energy in equal measure that I wanted more of.

Somewhat out of character, I decided to return the following year for one week *da sola,* on my own, and a second week with three friends from Canada. My vision for the visit was to practise my Italian and 'live like a local', and I knew it would be the perfect spot for both. Looking back, I wondered where I summoned the courage to show up at this distant place, to stay with someone I met over lunch. But events unfolded even more perfectly than I could have imagined.

It's hard to explain how profoundly that first week at Gatta Morena changed me. If I had to point to one experience in my years of travel through Italy that had the biggest single impact on me, that would be it. I did not have a car, so explored the area on foot, or with Tiziana when she invited me along. Although we had only met briefly, she took me under her wing like a sister. We ate together, either under the pergola or inside, in the middle of her bright, colourful kitchen. We went for hikes, rummaged around artsy towns, and visited her friends. She showed me historic highlights like a professional tour guide— Tarquinia, Tuscania, Parco di Vulci, and Capodimonte come to mind. I tried to help where I could; weeding the garden, picking little yellow *iperico* flowers that Tiziana used to make medicinal oils, and *fiori di sambuco* (elderflowers) that she used for syrup.

We spent free time under the pergola, often skimming fragrant lavender buds off their stems, later used to make yoga pillows and essential oils that Tiziana sold. Sometimes I was with Tiziana, or with her friend Chiara, or Elio, and we would chat away as we worked. Other times I was on my own, pleased to make a small dent in the bundles of dried flowers. Tiziana would tell me to relax; not to worry about dishes or sweeping the floor, or whatever little job I saw waiting for idle hands. I could not have felt more relaxed, but at the same time wanted to be a participant in life at Gatta Morena. These chores were a small contribution compared to the rewards I received by being there.

With Tiziana and Elio, and a basket of lavender.

The area was full of thermal springs and my host knew just where to find remote (and free) hot streams for a peaceful soak. I remember speeding down a country road one day, Chiara and Tiziana talking and laughing away as I sat in the back seat taking it in. They were speaking far too quickly for me to pick up much of what they were saying, but I loved every minute of it. I felt like I was witnessing the definition of friendship. We found a perfect spot just below the spa town of Saturnia to soak in a warm stream. Taking my cue from the others, I spread the mineral-filled mud from the stream bed over my torso and face, and we laughed at ourselves.

Further west was Terme di Saturnia, thermal springs that are open to the public. They are impressive just to look at from the road above, the steam rising as naturally hot water tumbles into layers of travertine pools covering this little piece of Tuscan countryside. The waters are rich in sulphur and other minerals and boast endless health benefits. On another occasion, Tiziana directed us to nothing more than an intersection of two country roads. The water was surprisingly hot, and no one minded that the location was not exactly four-star.

On one sunny day we drove to a country home near Marta, on Lake Bolsena, to visit an artist friend. The home was full of the artist's work, from unique sculptures to wall paintings. The elaborate garden surrounding the home included a huge labyrinth, an ancient symbol that relates to wholeness. Combining the image of a circle and a spiral into a 'meandering but purposeful path', they have long been used as meditation and prayer tools. Each spring, friends are invited to help re-paint this spiritual spiral, to give it new life. My visit that year coincided with this event, and I was pleased to be invited to join in. Chiara and I painted a *balena* (whale), my new word for that day.

Friends stopped by Gatta Morena frequently—to say hello, walk around the garden, discuss something they were planning. I recall many interesting people, such as a lady who restored ancient frescos utilizing paint she made from berries and other ingredients used in ancient times. Another friend was an engineer from Rome. I was fascinated to learn about the challenges he and his colleagues were facing during construction of a third metro line (Line C) across the Eternal City. Much of present-day Rome is built upon multiple layers that are rich in archaeological artifacts dating back well over 2000 years. Most of the work on the third line was far enough underground to be below these precious layers, but of course they had to come up to build the metro stations, ventilation shafts, and emergency exits. This is where complications arose.

The route upward runs through layers of history, even complete heritage sites in some cases. Work was constantly being halted as these archaeological treasures were encountered. A planned metro station in the centre of Rome actually had to be scrapped when it was found to be located over the Theatre of Pompey—an extensive site that is infamous as the location where Julius Caesar was killed. I have since learned that various sections of the line became operational between 2014 and 2018. However, the section under the heart of ancient Rome (arguably the most important portion from a mass transit perspective, given the volume of people it will serve) remains unfinished. I'd love to meet up with Tiziana's friend to learn about his work since I met him, over ten years ago.

Back to Gatta Morena. Tiziana would drop what she was doing when friends arrived and invite her visitors to sit and catch up over coffee or a cold drink. I could sense how her energy attracted positive energy and like-minded people. What I observed, and felt, really altered my thinking about how I wanted my life to look and feel.

On a rainy day in May, Tiziana invited friends over. Chiara brought her Tarot cards and we amused ourselves by, in turn, getting ours read. I remember the experience for assorted reasons. First, it didn't matter that this group of women did not all know each other, or that I did not know them. Everyone was friendly and warm, and together we found a way to make our own fun on a rainy Sunday afternoon. I enjoyed listening to the exchange of stories, and some lively singing along to old favourites. Each shared whatever they had to contribute in the way of food and wine.

I remember Chiara reading Tarot cards for a girl who worked in a bakery but desperately wanted to be a teacher. Chiara had turned a card that literally had a picture of a women baking bread, but graciously found a way to focus on more positive aspects of the story the cards were telling. When it was my turn, she first turned over the scales of justice. As a lawyer, it quickly caught my attention, although the meaning is more about balance than justice. From there, she said the cards suggested I was in a place of happiness and joy, which could not have been more accurate at that moment. I was immersed in a world that was light years from mine in many ways, yet still felt like home.

An instant connection emerged with Chiara from this experience, as if we had been friends for years. Working with her better English and my basic Italian, she spoke freely about her life, including some heartbreak she was going through. I have not crossed paths with many people like her, where the bond was as immediate or as deep.

At Gatta Morena with Chiara.

Speaking of Tarot cards leads me to the Giardino dei Tarocchi (Tarot Garden), a quirky place in Tuscany located just below the double-walled hilltop town of Capalbio. The garden is full of larger-than-life sculptures created by French artist Niki de Saint Phalle to represent the 22 major symbols of the

Tarot deck. Constructed of concrete and covered with bits of broken mirror and colourful ceramic, the pieces represent the artist's version of the mysteries of the Tarot. Besides the whacky sculptures, I noticed two Italian women sitting in a big teacup sculpture, mainly because they were laughing so much. I asked the ladies, who turned out to be good friends, if they would like their picture taken. The photograph turned out great, full of their big smiles. I forwarded it via email and was pleasantly surprised to receive a lovely response.

During my solo week at Gatta Morena, and on subsequent visits, I also enjoyed special conversations with Elio. Even though we didn't stay in touch between visits, it was wonderful to reconnect when I was there. On my last visit he asked me to join him for a drive, to catch up while he ran errands. We talked in Italian about nothing and everything. There was tension among the owners at this point. He didn't discuss the details, just the sadness, and how friendship and love and peace were more important than anything. The last I heard, he had sold his share in the property and moved back to Rome to care for his dying mother. I cried at the thought of him having to go back to chaotic Rome when I knew his heart was elsewhere.

I met Romolo, Elio's friend from Rome, the first year I stayed at the B&B. He spoke little English, and I didn't speak much more Italian back then. But somehow, we connected in a way that continues to amaze me. One afternoon when the two of us were lounging in the garden, we began talking at a progressively deeper level. We mused about family, the difference between loving someone and being in love, the evolution of relationships, and the freedom to be who you are and to do what you love. I remember thinking how crazy it was that I was talking about all these things with a virtual stranger, in a foreign language no less, and yet how comfortable and safe it felt. We were both married, and this absolutely had no sexual undertones. It simply did not feel like that, and yet I was filled with love for this human being. It was not unlike my experience with Chiara, and I wondered how it was that we can be moved so deeply by people we barely know.

On a return trip the following year, Romolo suggested we go for a walk. It was my pleasure. We followed the same path I usually took to Cellere, but the neighbour had locked a previously open gate along our route. What was one to do? Climb over of course. The small hiccup was that the owner's son appeared from the barn and made it abundantly clear that he was not impressed. The father came along as well. Having purchased olive oil from him, I assumed he would be more forgiving, but no such luck. Neither the father nor his rather aggressive son could offer a reasonable explanation for the barricade, but apparently it was their choice to make. There was tension, but Romolo kept his cool. Carrying on despite their scowls, we realised that our return trip just got longer. However, neither of us was in any hurry.

Further along, we had a much more amicable encounter with our friend Antonio, the old man who used to walk over to Gatta Morena for coffee. Sadly, his visits had effectively been cut off because of the locked gate. After a short stop, we left with our hands full of bounty from his garden. As our walk proceeded, I learned that Romolo and his wife had parted ways. They loved each other dearly, and their son, but were no longer in love. I am not certain if our initial talk was a precursor to how he was feeling,

Antonio on his garden tractor.

or just a coincidence, but it was endearing that he wanted to share his story. And even though we have not spoken since, the experience was a lesson for me about the nature of friendship.

I worked harder to stay in touch with Chiara. Before returning to Rome for our flight home one year, Gord and I took a little trip with Joe and Fil. Our tour included stops in Bolsena and Civita di Bagnoreggio (places I mentioned earlier) as well as the Umbrian city of Orvieto. This is home of the Well of St. Patrick (with its unusual double-helix stairways that allowed mules to carry water vessels down and up at the same time), the dominating fourteenth-century, black basalt and white travertine striped cathedral, a network of Etruscan caves below the city, and Orvieto's famous white DOC wines. Chiara continued to live in the area, so we arranged to meet over dinner in Bolsena.

I had not seen her for a few years, but with Christmas cards and social media, the connection continued to feel real. While the setting was pretty and the food delicious, the most delightful part of the evening was when I was trying to introduce my friends to Chiara and her friends. It was a unique situation to say the least, as Chiara's two guests were her ex-husband's fiancée and an ex-girlfriend. Chiara exclaimed in her charming Italian how lucky she was to have the people she loves still in her life. Everyone laughed, which set the tone for a relaxing and entertaining dinner. It was also another lesson about love.

I did not know quite how blessed I had been to experience Gatta Morena as I did until I stayed at a B&B in Apulia the following summer. I let myself believe I would find the same kind of emotional connection because it was owned and run by Tiziana's sister. Unfortunately, it quickly became apparent that this was a different world, in part because her sister had an entirely different personality, and because she and her husband also had a family business to run in town. While they were genuinely kind, dropping me off on their way to work when I needed a ride, and letting me use one of their bicycles, the relationship was impersonal. There were no long dinners under the pergola, or even chats over morning coffee. They brought out my breakfast, said good morning, and then retreated inside to get ready for work.

That said, it wasn't an unpleasant situation, just different. And through the differences I understood the reason I loved being at Gatta Morena so much. It was not because of the beautiful location, but the beautiful people, and the friendships I had cultivated there. Tiziana stopped taking B&B guests for a period when she and Pino moved onto their sailboat but they will always be in my heart. Then, I met Rosanna.

B&B Rosy in Campagna, Sardinia

In 2018 Gord and I began our Italian vacation in Sardinia. As an island, it was a less accessible region of Italy that I had yet to check off my list. I was pondering where we should base ourselves when a connection was again made through our friend Joe. He had met Rosanna while sailing and enquired about the possibility of her hosting us. She ran a B&B on the outskirts of Sassari, in northwest Sardinia. I prefer staying with someone who is not a total stranger, so the idea was appealing, We also fit the bill because she prefers to accept guests based on recommendations from friends. We worked out the details online, and the next thing I knew we were on our way to my nineteenth region of Italy.

Our plane was late arriving due to weather conditions over Europe, but Rosanna was patiently waiting. She has a big house with several guest bedrooms upstairs, and an attached apartment where we stayed. I especially loved our porch, where I could enjoy a morning coffee or evening sunset. The house is surrounded by a large acreage, including olive and fig trees. It is a peaceful location in the *campagna* (countryside) but close enough to town for convenience. I crashed as soon as I lay down.

The following morning Rosanna had thoughtfully put out a continental breakfast for us. And while we were technically on our own after that, she invited us to join her for several meals, kindly charging only our share of the cost of the food. The gesture was not expected but was certainly appreciated. It allowed us to connect, to enjoy the Italian lifestyle during our stay, and me to work on my Italian. Rosanna ate healthy fresh food, using in-season produce. Zucchini was clearly the veggie of choice during our visit. I was amazed at all the different dishes she came up with, from pasta with zucchini skin to zucchini bruschetta.

When travelling, I'm always looking for authentic experiences that I would not find back home. And as a guest, I like to contribute where I can. That too, adds to the experience for me. Noticing fig trees on Rosanna's property, we offered to pick some of the fruit. She gladly accepted and gave us baskets, clippers, and gloves for the task. We were instructed to handle them delicately, not to stack them, and to pick only the soft ones. Figs are easily bruised and, unlike other fruits, do not continue to ripen after they are picked. We managed to avoid getting the sticky white sap on our skin, for the most part, and ended up with enough for a batch of jam. As a child, I did not care for the texture of dried figs, but changed my tune when I discovered the sweet taste and soft texture of fresh figs.

In the afternoon I helped, or more accurately watched, as Rosanna made fig jam. She used only the ripe ones, avoiding any that were overly mature or bruised as they are more acidic and produce an inferior taste. We cut the tops off, then she cut the figs in half to make sure there were no insects inside before putting them in a pot to boil. Add fresh lemon juice and a couple of lemon rinds and stir frequently. When thickened, add sugar. I had to leave at this point, but the next morning I found a jar of fig jam on our doorstep. *Che bello!*

I also learned how to prepare olive trees for harvest. Rosanna had a young couple helping with the trees that year, so I offered to join them one afternoon. The physical work was good exercise, and I could practise my Italian while learning about a tradition that spans centuries. The olives were to be picked between the end of October and mid-January, but there were branches to be trimmed beforehand. This helps prevent tears in the nets that are placed below the trees to catch and collect the olives. The couple also explained that waiting for the olives to ripen and fall on their own usually meant they were overly mature and would produce oil of a lesser quality. Bruising would also create more unwanted acidity and a less pleasing flavour. Like wine, there are many details that go into determining the quality of olive oil—such as the soil and the position of the trees or vines (on a hill or plain), the weather of course, and how the olives are harvested and pressed—but it was interesting to learn a few of the basics.

That evening, Rosanna had me do a taste test to discover for myself the difference between the quality of her own olive oil and a mass-produced store-bought variety. I can't describe how much better hers tasted and smelled. I now understand why Italians are so obsessed with their olive oil. Even Rosanna's Italian dinner guests raved about hers.

I received a message and pictures from Rosanna several months later, ecstatic about her bumper olive harvest. I recall a similar message from Giovanni in Chianti following his exceptional olive harvest the same year. Both were so proud and excited. A lot of work was involved, but clearly it was rewarding.

Rosanna was genuinely interested in teaching us about Sardinian history and cultural traditions. On one road trip we stopped at Santa Sabina, a well-known *nuraghi* in central Sardinia. It was an opportunity for another history lesson. Considered to be one of the most archeologically advanced buildings of their time (the Bronze Age), nuraghi are included in the UNESCO World Heritage List. One of the best-preserved is the Barumini Nuraghe complex in central Sardinia, which has been carbon dated to 1478 BC. Today, these cone-shaped stone buildings are a symbol of Sardinia and its distinctive culture. More than 7,000 nuraghi have been found, though archaeologists believe there were over 10,000 at one time. There is no consensus on their function: they could have been the homes of local rulers, military strongholds, meeting places, temples, or a combination of these.

We also visited Orgosolo, a village in central Sardinia famous for its evocative murals that colour the streets. Created in 1969, the first mural commemorated the Pratobello Revolution, an uprising against the government's plan to create a military base and conduct dangerous testing on common land used by local shepherds. Following this event, Francesco Del Casino, a painter from Siena who moved to Orgosolo to teach art, took up the cause. He encouraged his students to create a series of murals to commemorate the thirtieth anniversary of Italy's Liberation.

Over time, the walls of the town have been decorated with hundreds of elaborate frescos in various styles of painting. The timeless murals speak to inhabitants and visitors alike, documenting Sardinia's cultural heritage, including the customs and traditions that reflect daily life and ongoing struggles for power and justice. Other themes include international political issues, such as the invasion of Iraq and the plight of immigrants. I was intrigued as we walked through town, even as I struggled to understand the Sardu writing and the story behind many of the murals. Luckily, we had Rosanna as our guide. And, as always, there were old men sitting on benches in the shade and children eating gelato.

The following year I returned to Sardinia on my own, hoping to spend time with Rosanna, practise my Italian, and learn more about the region and about life in Italy. Even though I had rented a car, Rosanna insisted on meeting me at the nearby Alghero airport. After an inefficient check-in process (to be kind), I finally got the keys to my rental car and followed her home. We chatted over a late lunch before I excused myself to settle into my apartment and catch up on some much-needed sleep.

The next morning, Rosanna asked in Italian if I were planning to do things on my own, or if I'd like to do things with her. She wanted to be clear. I responded just as clearly that I'd love to spend as much time with her as possible, doing anything she was interested in doing or showing me. That was all she needed to hear. From that point on, Rosanna treated me like a sister; we did almost everything together during my stay. I was in heaven.

We jumped right into action on my first full day, driving to Oristano, located about ninety minutes to the south, along the west coast of the island. Here we met up with Rosanna's friend Anna, and spent a rewarding day visiting historic sights. We started at Anna's with coffee and a local cookie favourite called *mostaccioli* and ended with aperitivo in Sant'Antioco as we watched the setting sun.

Enjoying an aperitivo in Sant'Antioco with Rosanna.

In between, we climbed to Torre San Giovanni di Sinis, admiring the views up and down the coast, and toured the nearby archaeological ruins at Tharros, a port city founded by the Phoenicians in the eighth century BC (possibly on the site of a much older Nuragic settlement). We visited a museum in Cabras that reinforced what we'd seen at Tharros and saw an exhibit on the Giants of Monte Prama (I Giganti). These enormous stone statues (up to 2.5 m high) were created during the Nuragic civilisation. While they date back to the eighth century BC or earlier, they were only discovered in 1974, guarding a grave site near Cabras. Between 1975 and 1979 over 5,000 pieces were recovered from at least 44 statues. Twenty-five statues have since been reconstructed and are now on permanent display at the museum.

Further south, to the charming island of Sant'Antioco (now linked to the mainland by a causeway), we toured the island, also rich with historical ruins dating to prehistoric times. One stop included the necropolis and tophet (an open-air sanctuary where ashes of children who died early or at birth were buried in urns) on the hill above the basilica. I was also fascinated by the *gruttas* (grottos or cave dwellings) built into the rocks around the island. They were designed initially as Punic tombs (in the late sixth century to the end of third century BC) and later adapted as houses for the poorer classes. Families continued to live in them until the 1970s, not unlike the Sassi cave houses in Matera.

All told, it was one amazing day, made even more enjoyable by the company of two lovely ladies, Rosanna and Anna.

I found Rosanna was like Tiziana in certain ways. Or perhaps I was just attracted to similar things in each of them. They have different personalities, but both are deeply knowledgeable and respectful of the history and cultural traditions of their regions. They also have enormous respect for the environment, doing their part to live sustainably. I have admiration and love for them both.

I've talked elsewhere about other things that Rosanna and I did together. In short, she exposed me to much more than I could ever have done on my own, and with a far deeper level of understanding. It was not just what we did and saw that was special, but little things like inviting me to share her meals, bringing me little homemade cakes and jam, helping me with my Italian, and inviting me to meet her friends. When I was getting ready to leave, her parting words in Italian were to the effect of, 'Next year, do not rent a car and stay for longer.' The pandemic has disrupted my short-term plans, but I fully intend to make that happen.

Delia, Sicily

Sicily is a unique region of Italy—its largest island and a world unto itself in many ways. Having been conquered by all the major powers of the day, its language, food, culture, art, architecture, and music each have layers of history captured within them. This story is about a special family I met there. Having absolute strangers welcome you into their home and treat you like family, simply because you are a friend of someone they know, was a heart-warming experience. This is precisely how we were treated in Delia. A small town of ancient origins, its name deriving from the Arab word for wine cultivation owing to the large presence of vineyards in the area.

My visit began when our Canadian friend, Joe D, heard we were planning a trip to Sicily. From there it was a done deal—we were staying with his Sicilian family. It was that simple for him. Joe's brother and mother lived in Delia, and his sister was going to be there as well, so it was going to be a family affair.

I was anxious about staying with a family I didn't know, but I recalled some travel advice I'd learned from Rick Steves. He encourages travellers to become extroverts. Not to wait passively for an experience to happen, but to reach out and make it happen. To stop and talk to locals, have coffee at the counter with them. To track down family and take everyone up on their offers. These, he explained, are the connections where you'll learn about local culture and traditions, and which will reveal a place's true character. So, even though my overactive brain was inventing reasons why we shouldn't bother them, in the end I accepted the offer. I'm sure Mr. Steves would not be surprised to learn that it was by far the most memorable aspect of my already memorable visit to Sicily.

Our hosts were waiting on the balcony when we arrived, and within an hour we were sitting out there with them, Lillo with his guitar in hand. I know from parties back home that Joe D loves to sing, and the passion clearly runs in his family. Music is such a lovely way to break down barriers, whether language or cultural differences, or just feelings of discomfort in a new situation. We shared meals and laughs, enjoyed a guided tour of their hometown, and exchanged stories about our excursions to nearby sights. These included the Valley of the Temples at Agrigento (a UNESCO World heritage site, famous for its well preserved Greek temples) and the white cliffs of the Scala dei Turchi (Turkish Steps, named after plundering Turks who took refuge here in ancient times) that nature has formed in the shape of a staircase.

Gord with Lillo on his balcony.

What has stayed with me most is how openly the family embraced us. I am ever grateful to them, and to Rick Steves for convincing me to ignore that little voice in my head. Before leaving we stopped to say good-bye to Joe D's elderly mom. We wanted a picture, but to get Gord in the frame he had to kneel. Even then, he was taller than she was. We all got a good laugh, and she had the biggest smile of all.

I'm reminded of a story from a woman I met in an Italian class. Her parents had died, and she longed to learn more about her roots. She'd never met her Italian family but was hesitant to reach out. I could certainly relate. When she did summon the courage to connect, they welcomed her with open arms, insisting she stay with them. She resisted initially, inventing excuses as I had. And while she may have arrived as a stranger, she left feeling like her family had grown exponentially.

CHAPTER 17

Around the Dinner Table

The Italian table serves as a stage for human drama.
Here people connect, reveal themselves, share pleasure,
satisfy curiosity, experiment, indulge.
—Elena Kostiukovitch

More so even than coffee, Italians connect over food. It is a major focus of their day. Like most Italians, our host at Il Colle felt that meals should never be eaten alone. I remember Giovanni saying that it was the worst thing ever if he had to eat alone; that he must have done something wrong. For him, food was to be savoured and enjoyed with family and friends. Luckily for Giovanni, his mother and grandfather both lived beside him, with the bonus that one or the other would always be doing the cooking.

Sitting down to a traditional family meal in Italy is more than just sitting down to eat. It is an event. I have also been treated to wonderful meals courtesy of our Canadian Italian friends. I recall one occasion when a younger friend made pappardelle with chestnut flour, a traditional pasta recipe from his wife's hometown of Genoa, in honour of her birthday. On other occasions, friends treated us to favourites such as home-made pizza, seafood soup, eggplant parmigiana, and various pasta dishes. But the food always seemed to taste better when I was eating it in Italy. I especially love the open-air dining that the climate supports. Below are a few of the highlights.

During our first visit to Fondi we were invited upstairs to eat with Joe's aunt and uncle. I was not prepared for the several courses that the lunch entailed, or how long it lasted. The same thing happened a few years later when I was in Fondi with a friend. Lunch was three courses, far more than either of us could eat, but the food was delicious, and we appreciated the effort. Just recently, when Gord and I were visiting, Zia Gina again insisted we come for lunch. She said it would be *un piacere* (a pleasure) to host us, and I could tell it was from her heart. She had a caregiver living with her to help with ailing Zio Paolo, and we were treated to a Moroccan-influenced chicken dish. Of course, there was pasta too. Gina is a tiny lady with an enormous heart, and a healthy appetite I might add. As she had done when we first stopped by, she thrust a bottle of her son's homemade wine into our hands when we were leaving. She assured us there was more where it came from.

Lunch with Zia Gina.

I found Zia Gina unusually talkative over lunch. Her husband, the only man she had ever loved, was suffering from severe dementia, and she wanted to reminisce. There had been talk of him being moved to a long-term care facility, but she explained that it simply would not work. Paulo would never stop calling for her if she were not there, and she would never let them move him away from her. She had been by his side for close to 60 years of marriage and his illness was not going to change that. As she became more emotional, Gina began talking faster, and much of her Fondi dialect was lost on me. But the emotion was clear. She was losing the love of her life.

It was also through our friendship with Joe and Fil that we got to know some of their friends, often around the dinner table. Maria Pia and Lucio, who I introduced earlier, live in a spacious home in Fondi, designed with separate apartments to house their entire family. Several memorable meals took place in their large garden, with some of their extended family gathered around a huge table. On one visit we were treated to a mini concert by their three granddaughters. The girls had rehearsed a trending pop song, but unfortunately the routine did not go as planned, with the youngest prancing around to the beat of her own drum. The production was charming, if not what the eldest had in mind. Maria Pia's multi-course meal, including *cozze e vongole* (clams and mussels), was hard to forget too.

At a local cafe in Fondi with friends: Filomena, SB, Maria Pia, Lucio, Gord, and Joe.

Their kindness extended beyond the dinner table as well. On an occasion when I was arriving in Fondi by train, and Joe and Filomena were in Canada, Lucio was happy to come and get me. Another time, he gave me a copy of a book that one of his son's had co-written, about learning to speak Italian—very appropriate! When I needed to see a hairdresser, Maria Pia made an appointment for me with her hairdresser. Then, she picked me up, drove me to the appointment, and came in to explain what I was looking for. She wanted to make sure that I was understood. I kept thinking that they barely knew me. But that was irrelevant. To them we were now friends, and those are things you do for friends. Today I could not imagine going to Fondi without stopping to see them.

Bruno and Luciana are other Fondi friends we met through Joe and Fil. When the four of us stopped by unannounced on one occasion, Bruno pulled extra chairs up to their table as if we had been invited all along. It didn't matter that they had dinner guests. Another year, when I was on my own, Bruno and Luciana insisted I join them and their daughter Virna for dinner. During that visit Luciana face-timed their other daughter, who was away at school, and the affection that flowed openly was something I was unaccustomed to.

Bruno, Virna and Luciana.

On our last visit to Fondi with Joe and Fil, we were invited to join Bruno and Luciana for a barbeque at their campground on the coast north of Gaeta. Their guests were an eclectic mix, including a man from Naples who brought a gorgeous, and delicious, *torta mimosa* for dessert. His suggestion was to start with a small slice as you will certainly want another. He was right. Filomena's eggplant parmigiana was also a hit. Dinner extended well into the evening, with Bruno on guitar for after-dinner entertainment.

The next year Gord and I stopped by the campground unannounced, just to say hello. It happened to be Bruno's birthday, and we were instantly invited to join them for dinner. I was hesitant, but Bruno was insistent. *Perchè vorreste andarvene?* (Why would you want to leave?), he asked. What could we say? We graciously accepted. Luciana had invited various relatives and friends and assured us there would be more than enough food. And there was. She had specialties delivered from nearby Gaeta, including pasta with *cannolicchi* (tiny shellfish typical of the area) and a huge platter of seafood. As Italians do, the courses were spread out over the evening and the intake of wine grew accordingly. Between courses, Bruno kept us entertained with his singing, accompanied by a guest on guitar. Everyone joined in.

Like Lucio and Maria Pia, even when Joe and Filomena were not with us, Bruno and Luciana made us feel welcome. When they were going to tour one of the campground guests around, Luciana extended an offer for us to join them. Do not bring anything, she said. We will stop on the way to get some things for lunch. Of course, when we did stop Bruno insisted on paying. I think Gord did manage to get him to share the cost, which made me feel a little better.

On the same trip we stopped in Terracina for coffee on the way home. Luciana wanted to find a restaurant along the *lungomare* (seafront) that friends of theirs owned. It was much more than a coffee shop, but their friends welcomed us all, served us coffee and desserts, and refused to accept any payment. Before they dropped us off, Luciana mentioned that a group from the campground would be going for dinner the following evening, at a place not far from Fondi. It was all going to be low-key, she said in Italian, and it would be great if we could join them. How could we refuse? And why would we want to? Impromptu experiences like these created some of my favourite memories.

I reminisce about meals at Gatta Morena over the years, a beloved location I have shared much about. A particularly memorable meal took place under the pergola when Romolo drove up from Rome with his wife and son, and Tiziana's good friend Chiara had also joined us. I was with three Canadian friends, and on our last evening we were being treated to pizza 'alla Romolo'. It was a lesson in the simplicity of Italian cooking. Homemade tomato sauce and dried oregano were the only toppings on one version, olive oil, fresh mozzarella from a local producer and *pomodorini* (little tomatoes) from the garden on another. Like my pizza margherita in the streets of Naples, the setting and company made the pizza taste even better.

I also remember this meal because of one special guest, Antonio. Even thought I had gotten to know him over several stays at Gatta Morena, he was an old *contadino* (farmer) and rarely ate anywhere but at home. Tiziana said that it was a big deal for him to go out, and he would be nervous. She suggested I ask him personally, knowing he would not refuse my invitation. His face beamed throughout dinner. It was obvious he loved being there. Gord and I dropped by Antonio's garden for a visit the last time we stayed at Gatta Morena, and he would not let us leave empty-handed, sending us on our way with eggs and a bag of other produce. His version of a hug and a kiss. I received sad news recently that Antonio's health has been failing. I am praying that I will be able to travel to Italy to see him soon, as it may be my last chance.

Around the table at La Casaccia, there were always greens and tomatoes from the garden for a self-serve salad, either a risotto or pasta or hot vegetable dish, and perhaps something left over from last night's dinner. We ate more lentils than I was used to, but I liked the way Elena made them. She was a great cook and found multiple uses for everything from the garden. Once she made risotto with thistles. Bizarre to me, but apparently full of nutrients. I loved that everyone stopped for lunch together, no matter how busy. Giovanni was *sempre tardi*, always late, but he always made it. Lunch was as much a part of their day as the work was, and they were equally committed to both.

While we had many pleasant meals together, by far the most exciting, and hectic, was a family gathering a few days after I arrived. Elena was hosting over forty family members, something she did once or twice a year. The meal was planned with precision, down to the tiniest details. First, after dinner one evening, the menu was discussed. She considered everything, from proteins and carbohydrates, to balancing heavier items with lighter dishes, and (most important for her) not too much sugar. So, despite the urging of Giovanni, there would be no gelato with the already sweet dessert. *Che peccato!* Too bad! She settled on three antipasti, including *vitello tonnato*, a classic Piedmontese dish of cold sliced veal (which she cooked the day before) and a creamy tuna puree. Then came the melt in your mouth *agnolotti* for the *primo piatto*, another regional favourite, *maiale e verdure* (pork and vegetables) for *il secondo*, and decadent chocolate-stuffed peaches for dolce.

Next was the grocery list. What did she have? What did she need? A big shopping followed, and then preparations began. I know I chopped more vegetables than I care to remember. I also learned how to make *pesce ripiene* (stuffed peaches). Elena's technique was impeccable; the peaches had to be perfectly level so the filling would not drip out or onto the fleshy orange ring around the top. She had a process for everything, but with that number of mouths to feed, and so many courses, organisation was the name of the game. It was exciting, but intense. And the intensity was turned up a notch on the day of the party when the guests started to arrive early!

With help from nieces and nephews, there was a production line for each course, from serving to collecting and washing dishes. Guests ranged from young to old, all grouped around temporary tables set up in the courtyard under large canvas tents. The heat was an issue, but guests rearranged their seats to avoid the hot sun as it moved across the cloudless sky. I was too busy in the kitchen to join the festivities outside, but the family ensured that a serving of each dish was set aside for me and the other staff to enjoy when we could. After coffee, dessert, grappa and other digestifs, the music began. One woman with an impressive voice entertained guests with several songs, including a version of 'Va Pensiero', the much-loved aria from Verdi's *Nabucco*, the unofficial Italian anthem. It was a wonderful ending to a wonderful meal.

A final story takes us back to my first visit to Sardinia. When Rosanna discovered that my birthday was the day before we were leaving, she quickly organised an impromptu birthday party. She invited friends, blew up balloons, and made a wonderful multi-course dinner, including *bottarga* (salted fish roe), a Sardinian delicacy. We also sampled three digestive liquors that Rosanna makes—one was *mirto* (a popular liqueur of Sardinia made with blueberry-like berries that grow freely in the countryside), one with grapes, and interestingly, one made with artichokes. The meal was topped off with a birthday cake and a rendition of *Buon Compleanno* (the Italian version of Happy Birthday). I was very touched.

One guest had brought her guitar along, so music followed (a theme in Italy, as you might have noticed). Rosanna also pulled out a strange-looking instrument called a *launeddas* (or Sardinian triple clarinet or triple pipe) that dates to at least the eighth century BC. It is a traditional wind instrument made of three long, thin pipes that are used to play two different melodies simultaneously. I should add that it is extremely difficult to get a sound out of this instrument, but Rosanna and her friends had fun trying. As the evening ended, I thanked Rosanna for her kindness. We didn't know each other well at this point, yet she wanted my birthday to be special. We shared coffee together the next morning and I left with an egg carton of fresh figs and *un abbraccione* (a big hug). I knew I would be back. And I was.

More research findings. Those who have more extensive social supports, whether through family, friends, or community created through organisations such as church, are more satisfied with their life. Further—another finding that was not surprising to me—those with higher life satisfaction levels value interpersonal relationships more than they do material goods. And what better way to build such relationships than around the dinner table? All the occasions I described, and others, added to my experience of the Italian lifestyle and helped to build lasting friendships.

CHAPTER 18

Something Smells a Little Fishy

Never does a man portray his character more vividly
than when proclaiming the character of another.
—Sir Winston Churchill

Travel is about experiences, and if you haven't had some disasters along the way, I would be surprised. I've certainly had my share. Here are some, where at least a lesson was learned.

After spending a few weeks on my own one year, a friend from Canada joined me. Visiting Gaeta one day, we lost track of time as we wandered along Serapo Beach and around the old town, and it was close to 2 p.m. before we began thinking about lunch. This is exactly when many places close for the afternoon, and not surprisingly, we had difficulty finding an open restaurant. We headed towards the marina where I thought we might have more luck, though it also guaranteed more touristy options. As we eyed a potential candidate, the manager cheerfully waved us in. I was sceptical, but our options were looking bleak. The grinning manager escorted us to a table and offered us wine. Without showing us a menu, he insisted that pasta would be *troppo pesante*, too heavy, for such a warm day. I looked around at the other tables, many with pasta plates, and my spider senses tingled again. His recommendation was a 'light' seafood salad as an antipasto, followed by a 'wonderful fresh fish', as he put it, mostly in Italian. Before I could say anything, my friend piped up, 'That sounds lovely.' The fact that she had just arrived in Italy and barely spoke a word of Italian seemed irrelevant.

We ended up with far more food than either of us could manage. It was also the most expensive lunch, perhaps meal, I have had in Italy. We were served two enormous plates of *frutti di mare* that included squid and octopus, marinated but uncooked. Not what my friend had expected, nor what she cared for. She did little more than push the squiggly creatures around her plate, and both plates went back largely untouched. We then tried to say that we were full, *piena*, *sazia*, and did not need the fish. 'Oh, but you must,' the manager insisted in Italian. 'It will be so good. And it is already being prepared just for you,' he added for good measure. In hindsight, I should have pulled out my Italian attitude and gotten up to leave, but we Canadese can be too polite.

While diners around us were enjoying their pastas and salads, out came our fish, heads and all. Again, not what my friend was anticipating. We picked some meat away from the bones, washed it down with the rest of our wine, and asked for *il conto per favore*. Even without fish bones in my mouth, I almost choked. I asked to see the menu (the one we should have been handed when we arrived) and realised that he had given us two servings of his most expensive antipasto, even though one could easily have fed two or more. He had also selected the most expensive fish he had on offer. Fish is sold *per etto* (100 grams), and I would not be surprised if he also served us the largest ones he had. In my friend's defence, she was extremely apologetic and insisted on paying the bill, but it was a lesson learned for both of us. Do not order anything without first seeing the menu or asking the price.

I had an all too familiar experience a few years later, this time on Elba Island with sailing friends, Debbie and Peter. At our request, a friend on the island recommended a good fish restaurant where he knew the owners. Sal even stopped there while driving us back to our boat, to point it out. The owners were not in yet, but we agreed to return for dinner, which we did, or so we thought. After being seated and wine glasses in hand, Debbie had a go at ordering in Italian. One waiter quickly turned into two, and the first was already collecting the menus as the second waiter said, '*Si, si,* I know what you want,' suggesting something in Italian that sounded like what Debbie had asked for. She thanked him for his help, and we thought nothing else of it—until the bill arrived. She had intended to order the grilled seafood platter, but what she had been served was a large grilled fish, at about twice the price.

Through the rear-view mirror, I'm quite certain these two clowns had run this little trick before. Now that I think about it, this type of thing may be a longstanding tourist scam. I recall my brother, years ago, having to argue with the waiter in a restaurant above Lake Como over something similar. What made it worse this time, was that we were at the wrong restaurant. We had gone into the first of two places that looked remarkably similar, but it was not the one Sal had recommended, sad to say. I have no doubt we would have had an entirely different experience at his friends' restaurant.

On Murano, an island in the Venice lagoon that is famous for the ancient craft of hand-blown glass, it was my sister who called out their scam. Her partner is a glass blower and Judy has learned a thing or two about the craft, including ways to identify factory-produced items. We had taken the vaporetto across the lagoon to visit the glass shops and watch what was billed as a glass blowing demonstration. The demonstration was comical, consisting of a man inserting a ball of molten glass into a red-hot fire and then twirling it around in the air while talking about the process. There was absolutely no glassblowing involved. At this point we assumed that the advertised 'demonstration' was merely a ploy to attract customers into their shop.

True to form, after the demonstration we were shepherded into the display area where they sold 'hand-made' products.

Everything looked pretty, but my sister was not impressed. She pointed to the smooth, flat-top openings of the vases, a clear indication, she said under her breath, that they were cut by machine rather than hand. I glanced up to see a store manager gazing at us. He took the liberty of explaining that the 'better quality' products were on display upstairs and asked if we wished to see them. We declined his offer. We hadn't intended to purchase anything, in part because we were living out of our suitcases, but also because authentic Murano glass can be extremely expensive, for good reason. The craft requires years of training to perfect the ancient art. Our enthusiasm had also waned at this point. It was a reflection on a sad reality. I later learned that much of the so-called 'Venetian glass' on display is mass-produced in Asia. On a brighter note, we continued to nearby Burano, known for the delicate lace produced on the island for generations, and enjoyed meandering through the streets with their colourful houses and shops.

Just one final story, so as not to dwell on the negative, as the good far outweighs the relatively few instances of questionable behaviour I experienced. This incident happened while we were on our way to a beach near Sperlonga, an area famed for its fresh mozzarella di bufala, and I wanted to get some for lunch. Popping into the shop on my own, I was clearly a tourist ready to be upsold (to be kind). I forget what he wanted to charge me for the ball of mozzarella that I had chosen, but I knew it was at least double the price it should be. I questioned the price, gave him a look to make it clear that I knew what was going on, and said thanks but no thanks. No cheese for our sandwiches today. I was disappointed but was not going to be taken for a ride because my accente was on the wrong syllable.

What La Dolce Vita is Really About

Twenty years from now you will be more disappointed by the things that you didn't do than by the ones you did. So throw off the bowlines. Sail away from the safer harbor. Catch the trade winds in your sails. Explore. Dream. Discover.

— H. Jackson Brown Jr.

La dolce vita literally means 'the sweet life', evoking the notion of living life to its fullest, however that may look for you. The famous 1960 film, *La Dolce Vita*, directed and co-written by Federico Fellini, was a shocking, satirical play on this theme, and an incongruous title for a film that championed a superficial materialistic lifestyle. The film follows a journalist on a seven-day journey through Rome in a futile search for happiness. It can be seen as a metaphor for life—the notion that what we think will make us happy often is not what does; that our view of the sweet life may in fact be an illusion.

I'm quite sure I had no idea what I was looking for when I started my travels through Italy years ago, or if I even had a set goal. Certainly, there were many wonderful experiences to be had, stunning places to see, amazing meals to be enjoyed, wine to be savoured. But whatever I may have been looking for, I did not find it in anything close to Fellini's version of 'the sweet life'. Rather, it was in the relationships I built and the connections

I made, sometimes with complete strangers, that impacted me most deeply and gave me the most joy. These connections often happened when I was participating in traditional Italian activities, such as aperitivo, passeggiata, and sagre, or enjoying dinner around a big Italian table. I believe that the more we get to know others, the more we come to know our own truth; our own 'sweet life'. And for me, it was with the benefit of hindsight that lessons were learned, and my truths were revealed.

I have long recognised that my brother has an innate ability to enjoy life, whether through food or drink or music or hiking or biking, always choosing to engage with others along the way. I recall getting annoyed at times when we were travelling together because he was lingering too long over his after-dinner drink or chatting up the servers when I was ready to leave. Perhaps his years in Switzerland and time spent absorbing the rich European culture enhanced his ability to wring the most out of life. It took me many more years to appreciate how to savour the moment, and I attribute that to a significant degree to my time in Italy. Those years helped me learn valuable lessons about the fundamentals we all need for happiness, and my version of the sweet life. And many of those lessons came when I was either forced to, or chose to, connect with others.

I continue to cycle back to words of wisdom from Rick Steves, who refers to Europe as 'a cultural carnival', where the best acts are often free and where spending more money may only build walls between you and what you came to see. I didn't necessarily have much money to spare for most of my travels through Italy, and I do believe my experiences were richer for it. Steves also offers the concept of travel as 'life intensified', suggesting that it broadens our perspective and teaches us new ways to measure quality of life. True to his word, my most meaningful travel experiences have often been the result of unplanned events, unexpected encounters, and taking the road less travelled. It is a truism that travel changes us; but if we are not prepared to veer off the beaten path, we are unlikely to meet anyone except other tourists and the transformational opportunities will be lost.

I have a few regrets in this regard. One involved a Mediterranean cruise. At the urging of friends, I had agreed to join them on a short cruise that started and ended in Italy. One of the stops was Kusadasi on Turkey's Aegean coast—the closest port for an excursion to the nearby city of Ephesus. This was the most important city in the Byzantine Empire next to Constantinople, and home to an early Christian community from the middle of the first century AD. The Gospel of John may have been written here, and the ruins of a sixth-century church, the Basilica of St. John, believed to have been built over the Apostle's tomb, can still be seen today.

On our return from Ephesus, we were dropped off at a large outdoor market near the port. I had been excited to do some shopping in the market, but quickly lost interest for some reason, and opted to head back to the ship early. After moving away from the crowds, I encountered a man who was sitting on a stool, quietly enjoying what I learned was apple tea. He spoke some English and we struck up a conversation of sorts. Then he asked if I would like some tea. I graciously accepted and waited as he went inside a canvas tent. But as I waited, I managed to talk myself out of it, imagining that somehow things would not end well. I attracted his attention and said I was sorry, but I had to go, that I would be late, and promptly left.

I left because of my fears; because of the stories I invented. I went back to the ship and waited for my shopaholic friends to join me. It was a regret because I could have stayed and talked to him, even if I didn't try his tea. It was a regret because it was an opportunity lost. It was also a lesson learned.

Throughout this book I have focused on aspects of Italian life that left an indelible mark on me. Many are simple parts of everyday life that an Italian might take for granted. But as an outsider making my way through Italy, often with no fixed itinerary, these everyday habits, rituals, and traditions had a profound effect on how I experienced the country. My wish is for you to see these things as I did—as vehicles for connecting with people and cultivating the sense of belonging that we all crave.

And thanks largely to our dear friends Joe and Filomena, and a little bravery on my part, I now have a family of friends across Italy who are at the real heart of Italy for me. Those relationships revealed Italy to me in a way that would not have otherwise been possible, an Italy I would not have discovered on my own. And they forever changed me in the process. Italy opened its doors to me and I chose to walk through—and my life is richer for it.

Writing this, I can't help thinking about Anthony Bourdain and his show, *Parts Unknown*, which I loved, loved, loved. He drew people together over simple, traditional food, and would often get them to bare their souls while slurping noodles from plastic bowls. Through his travels to every corner of the globe, and over many conversations across makeshift dinner tables, he highlighted not only the amazing diversity this world has to offer, but also the common elements that connect us all, no matter where we live—our common humanity. There were many lessons to be learned.

Looking through the rear-view mirror, I see the truth behind Bourdain's legacy and have begun to understand how it encapsulated the essence of what my travels had been revealing to me: lessons about stepping outside our comfort zone to pursue our dreams; about the importance of human connection (now more than ever); about how something as simple as a coffee or an aperitif can be a facilitator for human interaction; and how simple connections can feed our souls.

So, what are those universal constants? The ones that Bourdain seemed to discover in his extensive travels, and that I slowly began to understand from mine? The social connections that Susan Pinker and others argue meet our most fundamental universal needs? While I do believe it is through our own journey that we derive the greatest benefit, I also believe that these universal needs, or constants, will lead us to the same place if we let them. We are all hungry for the same things. To be seen and heard. To be valued for who we are, flaws and all. To matter. To have hope and purpose. To be given space and time to experience life to the fullest. To live our passion. To love and be loved.

Regardless of where the experiences took place, the most memorable for me were differing versions of these common themes. They included examples of being welcomed as I am, living in community, bonding over common pleasures and ancient rituals, sharing joy and pride in something bigger than ourselves. Although I didn't recognise it at the time, they were the examples of 'living life in the piazza' that pulled me back to Italy again and again. My experiences introduced me to a country and its people who worship family, good food, and tradition, who crave connection and a sense of community—some of the universal constants that exist in every corner of the world.

Maybe this is the stuff that la dolce vita is truly all about. *Chissà?* Who knows? It isn't that my Italian experiences could not have taken place elsewhere. Of course, they could. But Italy was the vehicle that intensified my life, and ultimately made it much sweeter.

REFERENCES

Brown, Brené, *Braving the Wilderness: The Quest for True Belonging and the Courage to Stand Alone*. New York: Random House Publishing Group, 2017.

DiTommaso, A. Ghigo, 'Here's How American Cities Can Learn from Italian Piazzas,' *Next City* (blog), April 16, 2015, https://nextcity.org/daily/entry/italian-piazzas-the-future-of-public-space

Hales, Dianne, *La Passione: How Italy Seduced the World*. New York: Penguin Random House, 2019.

Herzog, Werner, 'The World Reveals Itself to Those Who Travel on Foot', interview by Peter Gwin, *National Geographic*, August 26, 2020, https://www.nationalgeographic.com/travel/2020/08/werner-herzog-interview-on-bruce-chatwin-film-nomad/#close

Hudson, W.H., *Idle Days in Patagonia*. New York: E.P. Dutton & Company, 1926.

Hugger, Dan, 'Economic Lessons from Thoreau's 'Walden,'' Acton Institute Blog, March 3, 2019.

Iacopelli, Roberto, (Dolomites Mountain Guide), 'Roberto's Dolomites Information: Info 3', Discoverydolomites.com (blog), https://www.discoverydolomites.com/wordpress/wp-content/uploads/2016/08/INFO3_survive.pdf

Lieberman, Matthew D., *Social: Why our Brains are Wired to Connect.* New York: Crown, 2014.

Marron, Catie, ed., *City Squares: Eighteen Writers on the Spirit and Significance of Squares Around the World.* New York: Harper, 2016.

Oprah's Super Soul Conversations, 'Dr. Alan Lightman: How to Lead a Less Hurried Life', May 6, 2020, https://omny.fm/shows/oprah-s-supersoul-conversations/dr-alan-lightman-how-to-lead-a-less-hurried-life

Oprah's Super Soul Conversations, 'Howard Schultz: Pouring Your Heart into Your Business', September 14, 2017, https://www.youtube.com/watch?v=ltkJ5mGHd1I

Pinker, Susan, *The Village Effect: How Face-to-Face Contact Can Make Us Healthier and Happier.* Toronto: Vintage Canada, 2015.

Roden, Claudia, *The Food of Italy.* London: Arrow, 1990.

Schultz, Howard, with Joanne Gordon, *Onward: How Starbucks Fought for Its Life without Losing Its Soul.* New York: Rodale, 2011.

Steves, Rick, 'Rick's Travel Philosophy', *Rick Steves' Europe* (blog), https://www.ricksteves.com, https://www.ricksteves.com/press-room/ricks-travel-philosophy

Webb, Christine, 'An Italian Institution – the Piazza', *ITALY Magazine*, May 23, 2008.

Yiruma, 'River Flows in You', https://www.youtube.com/watch?v=7maJOI3QMu0

CPSIA information can be obtained
at www.ICGtesting.com
Printed in the USA
LVHW080402010223
738390LV00010B/402